D1128227

Dog Training
for Law Enforcement

R.S. Eden

Detselig Enterprises Ltd.
Calgary, Alberta

Dog Training
for Law Enforcement

R.S. Eden

Canadian Cataloguing in Publication Data

Eden, R.S. (Robert S.)
    Dog training for law enforcement

ISBN 0-920490-47-6 (bound). — ISBN
    0-920490-48-4 (pbk.)

1. Police dogs — Training.   2. Dogs — Training.
I. Title.
HV8025.E33 1985   636.7'0886   C85-091095-1

Second Printing November 1986
Third Printing November 1987

© 1985 by Detselig Enterprises Limited
P.O. Box G 399
Calgary, Alberta T3A 2G3

SAN 115-0324
Printed in Canada   ISBN 0-920490-47-6 (hardbound)
                            0-920490-48-4 (paperback)

About the Author

Robert S. Eden was born in Calgary in 1956, and has been training dogs, both professionally and privately, for ten years. A police constable for the past five years, Eden is currently serving with a Canadian police force, and has been a member of the Canadian Police Canine Association since 1979. He is married and has one child.

Disclaimer

While every effort has been made to ensure that the methods and recommendations contained in this book are sound and accurate, the results of dog training vary with each dog and handler, and with the unique circumstances of any particular incident. Neither the author nor the publisher accepts any legal or moral responsibility nor any liability for the outcome of any case or incident, nor for any errors or omissions.

I have read Bob Eden's *Dog Training for Law Enforcement* and I believe it will be of benefit to a police department intending to set up a K9 unit, to one which wishes to improve its existing unit or to a handler who wishes to upgrade his own skills. This book also gives the reader an in-depth view into the values of a K9 Unit.

Bob's knowledge of and enthusiasm for police dogs shows through in this manual. While I may not agree with everything he has written, I respect his convictions. This is a book which needed to be written; it is one of the few police K9 manuals written by a policeman for policemen. Even if an experienced trainer and/or handler finds only one or two exercises which help refine his training skills, then, in my opinion, this book has been successful.

I believe Bob intends to write a more detailed technical manual for the advanced trainer/handler, and I look forward to studying it as well.

Sgt. Rick Fackrell
London Police Dog Section
London, Ontario

I have read your manuscript and feel for the first time a book has been written which will be of enormous value to the Police Officer who wishes to become involved in the world of the Police Canine. Keep up the good work.

J.A. McDonald, Master Trainer
Pierce County Sheriff's Department
Tacoma, Washington

As a police officer and active K-9 handler, I can honestly say this is the most informative general purpose book about the K-9 I have ever read!

Officer Robert Willey
K-9 Handler
Centralia Police Department
Centralia, Washington

To Grandma Fergi and "her dog," with love.

Acknowledgements

I wish to offer my sincere thanks to the following people for their assistance in putting this work together:

Officer Bob Willey, Dogmaster, Centralia Washington Police Department.
Deputy Jack Macdonald, Head K9 Training Officer, Pierce County Sheriff's Office, Tacoma, Washington.
Sergeant Rick Fackrell, Head Training Officer, London Police Dog Section, London, Ontario.
Dr. David Huff D.V.M., Huff Animal Hospital, Tsawwassen, British Columbia.
Sergeant Rick Wilkes and the Edmonton City Police Department, Edmonton, Alberta.
Constable Brian Amm, Dogmaster, and the Calgary City Police Service, Calgary, Alberta.
Herr Peter Backmann, Head Training Officer, Zurich Police Dog Section, Zurich, Switzerland.
Inspector Robert Velecky, Customs Detector Dog Service, Department of National Revenue, Canada.
Washington State Police K9 Association.
Sergeant Randy Pond, West Valley Police K9 Section.
Officer Brooke Plotnick, West Valley Police K9 Section.
Officer Craig Gibson, West Valley Police K9 Section.
Officer Jim Crowley, West Valley Police K9 Section.
West Valley City Police Department, West Valley, Utah, U.S.A.

Ruth-Anne Eden.	Bryce Karl.
Scott Hoadley.	Rick Joncas.
Dave Roberts.	Dave Pawson.
Ian McLellan.	David and Gail Hamilton.
Dorian Boswell.	Doug Sales.

Photo Credits: *London Free Press*, London Ontario; Dave Roberts A.R.P. S.; Scott Hoadley; Jack McDonald; Quinn Orr; *The Western Review,* Drayton Valley, Alberta. Cover photo by Quinn Orr

Artwork: Mike J. Woodcock

Detselig Enterprises Ltd. appreciates the financial
assistance for its 1987 publishing program from

Alberta Foundation for the Literary Arts
Canada Council
Department of Communications
Alberta Culture

Contents

Introduction

This book is written with two purposes in mind. First, it is intended as a basic guideline for the law enforcement officer on the street who requires a partner he can depend on in any life-threatening situation. It is far from complete in this respect, but if followed step by step, the book will produce a K9 team capable of handling most situations encountered in police work. Street survival situations are discussed to a limited extent, but because the book is also designed for use by the general public, such specialties as drug enforcement, explosives detection, hostage dogs and Emergency Response Team applications have not been included. It is hoped that as this book proves useful to those in the law enforcement field, particularly to those agencies just starting out their own dog units, subsequent supplements in these specialties will become available exclusively to law-enforcement agencies. I will provide the basics of dog handling which are vital to your survival on the street. Once they are learned it is up to you, the officer, to apply these principles, to continue the task of training, and to improve your level of performance.

The second purpose of this book is to provide instruction for the general public on how to raise and train a dog to be both a reliable protector and a trustworthy companion. Goals for this type of training include personal protection by the use of gradually escalating threats to the offender and the use of direct attack if, and only if, it is absolutely required. However, this animal must also be a companion who is gentle with children of any age. He will respond instantly to softly-spoken commands in any situation and will be capable of living within the family unit without having to be constantly corrected. He will be loved for his dedication, will be a child's playmate, and will become the ultimate jogging companion.

Most dog training books I have encountered do not include problems directly related to the law enforcement field. Others include confusing information which may be required by trainers of specialty dogs, but which is unnecessary for our purposes. This book is written from a police officer's point of view. It is also written from the viewpoint of a family man with children, who depends on his K9 friend to protect them in his absence. Only those points have been included which are necessary to produce a police service or personal protection dog of excellence.

For those who are new to the field of dog training, the text will instruct you in an easy-to-understand sequence not just how to train your dog, but to understand and communicate with him. The book is designed to teach you about your dog, and then to assist you in developing the traits you desire for him.

For those in the field of law enforcement, the text will prepare you and your partner for what is commonly known as General Duty. It includes every aspect of police service dog basic training, and filters out a lot of the unnecessary text which is often included in department manuals. The information on scent, the dog's sense of smell, and his anatomical makeup is all directed to the use of the dog in law enforcement. Though the methods taught are basic, they have proven very effective in the field. This is a first edition, and further additions to the text will come in subsequent publications as new methods and results are found. The knowledge put into this book is an accumulation of seminars, courses, studies, and experiences I have encountered. I feel I am just beginning to learn about our canine friends, but I want to pass on what knowledge I have to those who, together with their partners, wish to strive for performance excellence.

1

1
Starting Out

The dog has long been considered man's closest companion. He has protected livestock, property and families; he has gone to war as a fighter, and been trained as a rescuer. In most recent years he has been the close companion of many police officers working the streets.

In this capacity he is a companion, a protector, a tracker of both lost children and violent criminals. He is used to apprehend armed and dangerous subjects but is also taken into schools and allowed to mingle with the children. There is no greater responsibility given to any beast than that of the protection of people living within the community in which he works.

This book will strive to produce such an animal. The author is extensively familiar with the German Shepherd breed and the experiences related are therefore from encounters involving the Shepherd. Those wishing to train other breeds will find little or no adjustments required to accomplish the training goals.

The breeds preferable for training may vary, depending on the department's requirements. The best all-purpose general duty dog accepted worldwide is the German Shepherd. However, the Rottweiler, Doberman Pinscher and Bouvier des Flandres are also excellent working dogs. Bloodhounds have always been the top tracking dogs, and black Labs are proving to be very successful as drug and bomb-detection animals.

Keep in mind that you may not want a heavy-coated animal if you are working in a hot climate, and you wouldn't want to be using a Doberman in northern Canadian regions in mid-winter. In this respect your choice of dog has to be tailored to the climate of your area as well as to duty requirements.

Each individual dog has a personality, and as such must be viewed and chosen for his individual abilities. My present line of Shepherds are descendants of the "Quanto Von Der Wienerau" line. This, as some readers will know, is a line bred for showdogs and is not considered tough enough for Schutzhund or police work. (This is what I have been told during my visits to various Schutzhund clubs.) I have hand-picked my partner, his brothers and sons for training as police service dogs and each has excelled in his work. Breeders will argue as to who has the "best" line, yet this example demonstrates that the individual dog must be chosen for his own traits as well as for his background. Choose your candidate first for temperament, then test him for his potential in the field for which you are preparing him.

A dog which is rated excellent as a tracker and protector is nonetheless a poor candidate if he is of poor temperament.

Whatever breed you choose, this book will give you a better understanding of how the dog thinks, works, and how he relates to people. Follow it in sequence and take the time to read the chapters prior to the training sessions, as they will help you to properly analyze your particular situation and make you conversant in the ways of your dog. The period of time normally required to adequately complete the course is twelve weeks. This will vary, depending upon the frequency and duration of sessions, as well as upon the individual dog, but at the end of this time your dog should be well-controlled and nearing the completion of training.

If you are a law enforcement officer, you should remember that you are not looking for an attack dog. You are after a precision animal that can be controlled and directed at your every whim — an animal to whom you can entrust your life in the most dangerous of situations. Take the time to learn the basic principles step by step. The better you understand and communicate with your partner, the safer and more capable you will be as a law enforcement team.

Administration can sometimes be a major obstacle to the development of the dog unit, particularly with reference to budget considerations and inadequate knowledge of the ever-changing science of dog training. Methods of breeding, raising and training police service dogs change continually as we learn more about the animal's capabilities. It is up to you as a street level officer to assist the administrators by telling them your problems and teaching them the idiosyncracies of a dog team.

Some departments experiment with new methods of training in an attempt to decrease training time, or with theories such as rotating the dogs to new handlers every few years in order to promote officer career development. Both of these are direct routes to poor production and eventual failure by the dog squad. There is no short cut to training. It is a long and concentrated effort on the part of the dog and the handler, which should be carried out in proper sequential order to ensure maximum control in each training phase before progressing to the next.

Officers should be chosen who wish to remain as dog handlers for at least the life of their dog, as only teams which truly understand each other will produce optimal results.

Departments which incorporate mandatory rotation will encounter situations where a handler loses interest as he nears the end of his mandatory rotation period. He has been asked to dedicate himself totally to his dog, has grown to love him, and administration then requires that he break that bond at the end of a specified mandatory rotation period. As that time nears and the handler prepares to break the bond with his partner, he gradually spends less time with the dog and tries to lose interest in an effort to alleviate the hurt and anxiety one encounters when losing a close friend. Apprehension rate and the quality of work deteriorate as the officer, along with his family, prepares to lose a close family member. This is not fair to the department, to the handler and his family or to the dog.

This is not to say that teams which are rotated, or which are put through training that attempts to teach all aspects such as obedience, tracking, and aggression from the first week, will not succeed. Those responsible will have dogs that are successful in their eyes, yet many animals which would be excellent for the job given proper sequential training are scratched from the courses and the fault is said to lie entirely with the incapabilities of the dog. The results of the teams graduating from these courses as opposed to proper sequential training become obvious. The dogs are lacking in proper control and have only a small percentage of the apprehension rate they could have had if the proper training procedures had been implemented.

If you are just starting a dog squad, be sure to look around and examine the results from various training facilities before going into training.

The public also has various ideas or misconceptions about the trained service dog, and again it is up to you to bring this image forward in a positive manner. A professional dog team doing demonstrations in schools and at various public functions both acts as a deterrent factor, and wins public support from citizens of all ages by showing that the dog is a precision working animal which is actually very gentle and loving unless other circumstances require his aggression.

There are different methods of training dogs and different breeds of dogs which every breeder feels is the best for the job. Only you can decide what is best for your needs. The methods which I have incorporated into the following chapters are ones that have always worked for me in the training of precision police service dogs which are gentle and trustworthy within my home. I do not accept failure, and any dog I have chosen to take through this training has always completed it with a very high level of success. It is the best I have to offer in the way of a basic manual. Whether it helps you to understand your K9 partner better or whether you learn only one small hint that improves your abilities as a team, then I have succeeded in my endeavors.

2

2
Pack Instinct

This chapter will enable you to understand the socialization patterns of your dog. To really comprehend and be able to communicate fully with your partner you must first learn to think as he does. This requires an understanding of his basic instincts.

All canine species have a definite pack structure, with each animal in the pack having a specific social rank. The leader of the pack is the Alpha male. In the wild he is the most aggressive male and can be forced out of his position only by strong aggression. He is the sire of the pups in the pack with rare exceptions, and is responsible for pup survival. He is constantly challenged for his position by the Beta male, but remains secure in his position as the "boss" as long as he remains the strongest.

The next rank in the pack is the Alpha female. She, along with the Alpha male, is responsible for raising as many pups as are required to sustain the pack. She will be the prime producer of pups, occasionally mating with members of the pack other than the Alpha male, and preventing the other females of the pack from reproducing.

Next in line is the Beta male. He is the most likely successor to the Alpha male and is constantly challenging and testing him. He is usually related to the Alpha male or Alpha female and will on occasion mate with the Alpha female.

They are followed, in order, by low-ranking males (who are usually independent and will often form new packs with other low-ranking members), then low-ranking females, the juvenile members and finally the pups.

This pack structure is important to us in that your new puppy, as he grows into adulthood, will view other members of your family in terms of this socialization.

In a family where the dog is being raised as a police service dog (PSD), it is very important that he be allowed to maintain the position of a Beta male. The handler will be the Alpha male and his wife becomes the Alpha female. If one understands the pup's socialization pattern, this will assist the family raising the PSD to maintain the dog's confidence and social position.

Should every member of the family attempt to dominate the dog and he is not allowed to maintain his position, his confidence may wane, causing severe problems for the prospective police or protection dog. This does not mean the dog should be allowed to do anything he wants, nor that the children of the family cannot give him commands, but the majority of commands and corrections should be given by the handler.

Bonding

Feeding, grooming, and play are also important in this socialization process. While playing with the pup, let him win once in a while, whether it be tug of war or just wrestling around. This allows him to build and maintain his confidence and cements a strong bond between dog and handler.

The importance of this bond cannot be stressed enough, particularly in the PSD. It takes many hours of work, play and constant companionship to build that bond.

The dog should be regarded as your best friend, closest partner and on-the-job companion. He is not to be treated as a pet which would relegate him to a low position on the pack social scale. The officer must have a genuine love for the animal and the dog must be allowed to display the same affection to his handler. He will do this by playing, staying close, or even by working harder. A well-bonded dog lives to hear praise from his master and will do anything to obtain it. This is the key to training and can only be achieved by officers who are dedicated to working with their new four-legged partner for the lifetime of the dog. This bond should never be broken in attempts to retrain the dog for another handler unless it is absolutely necessary. One risks breaking the dog's spirit and motivation by suddenly removing him from his life-long social structure in his family and forcing him to learn new ways and to try to fit in with the social structure of a new family; this is a chance that is simply too great to take.

The bond between them provides a great asset to both dog and handler: they learn to read each other's actions. This can often take the better part of a year to accomplish, but a dog team which appears to have total understanding is a fascinating thing to witness at work. In my own experience, for example, my dog indicated a suspect in an alley by frequently turning his ear back. He was sent to apprehend a second suspect while I turned the corner behind us to check his indication; I found the suspect lying under some stairs. This occurred in the black of night with only a flashlight for lighting, but with a dog I understood and could read, I was able to locate a suspect who under usual circumstances would have gone undetected.

In another instance, we were working a stakeout on a drug drop where, due to the location and a suspect who was wise to surveillance, it was impractical to utilize sufficient manpower to cover the area. Therefore my partner and I were positioned on our own inside the target area and I used the dog's natural abilities to my advantage. As the night progressed my dog suddenly lifted his head, ears intently forward, and quite obviously indicated that someone I couldn't see was walking across the site. His head slowly panned left to right as he focused on the sound of the suspect's footsteps and movements. At this point backup was called to contain the area. We closed on the suspect and the apprehension was made. By using the dog's abilities to avoid the high-visibility surveillance to which the suspect was attuned, we successfully concluded this incident.

This very simple yet creative use of the dog's abilities demonstrates the benefits to be derived from clear understanding between dog and handler. Take the time to work on the bonding process and learn to use his attributes and body communication to your advantage; it won't be long before you will be able to read and anticipate what your partner is going to do, and understand why, even before he acts.

3

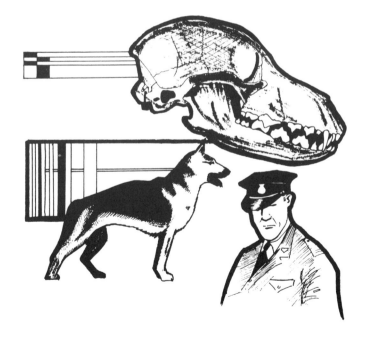

3
Reading
and Understanding
K9 Behavior

The primary role of the K9 officer is to read properly and evaluate his dog's body language. This phenomenon of canine communication enables the officer to utilize his animal's ability to sense things, to read very subtle clues from the dog's behavior, and to detect things which are often overlooked. Different ear directions, for example, can warn the officer of two different suspects, each of whom is heard by the dog. The dog can work on only one suspect, but if read properly before the dog acts, the signals can often warn of hidden dangers.

Whether you are a law enforcement officer or someone training your dog as a jogging companion for personal protection, this canine behavior can make the difference between success and failure during your training. Fully understanding your dog and his actions enables you to communicate with him as friend and partner rather than as merely a handler with a trained animal.

There are various aspects to language behavior which may occur separately or in combination. These signals, properly read, will tell the handler everything he needs to know in a given situation. This is particularly important during training. If you misread your dog's physical signs you may unknowingly correct him or guide him at the wrong times. For example, if you attempt to teach the dog to track before you have taken the time to complete obedience training, you may very well fail as the dog does not yet understand the basic movements required for control during tracking phases.

By starting with basics and taking the time to perfect them, you form a bond. The dog learns to understand your particular style of command and movement, and at the same time you learn to read your dog's reactions. As the bond strengthens the animal will have a better understanding of what you require of him, and he will pay particular attention to you, and try harder to please you. This attentiveness comes naturally during the first phases of training. Therefore, although it can be done, do not attempt to combine different phases of training until you have mastered your basics and both of you are fluent in your abilities. This will very likely prevent the task of looking for a more "suitable" animal when in fact your animal was more than adequate. Without realizing it you may fail to instill the attentiveness and perseverence in him which the basics are designed to do. Therefore, go step by step and learn to read your partner very carefully. Learn the various language components.

The first of these components is the dog's eyesight. It is a common belief that the dog has poor and limited vision. On the contrary, although they may see differently than we do, tests have shown that dogs can focus very clearly on objects at a distance of over 100 yards. They can, in fact, see as clearly as we do, although it is uncertain whether they can distinguish colors.

The animal's keenness of sight can be sharpened by simple games such as throwing a ball. The dog can see and identify articles or suspects which move, even at considerable distances, and it is believed that canine night vision far exceeds that of human beings. This ability to see slight movement is the aspect of sight used most by the dog.

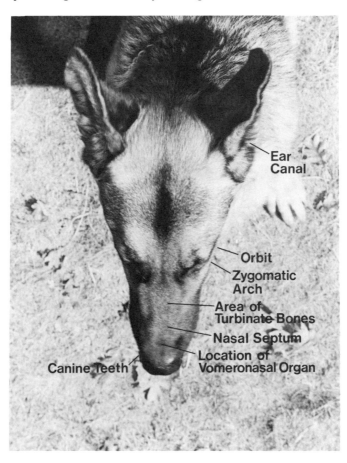

The second component is the animal's keen sense of smell. To understand fully this seemingly phenomenal ability we should first examine how the animal's olfactory system is built.

Looking at the dog's nose, it would appear that it is built with two long tubes for nostrils. Each nostril is, in fact, full of scroll-like passages which are lined on both sides by millions of receptor cells. These scroll-type receptors are called the turbinate bones and are built into the upper part of the nasal area. The air inhaled by the dog moves into the upper part of the nasal area through the turbinate bones. This allows the dog to distinguish specific scents. The olfactory system of a human being is approximately one inch in area, as compared to that of a dog which can be close to one yard in area. The dog also has a powerful ability to store and recall scents from memory. This will be discussed in more depth as we progress.

The sense of hearing is the next aspect of behavior language to which

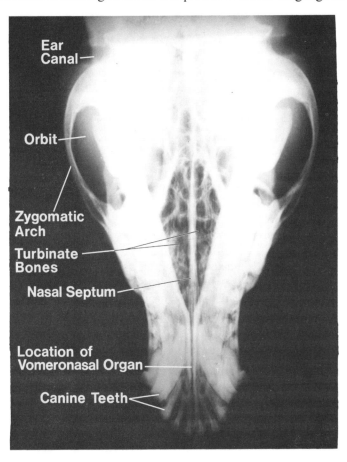

we must pay attention. Sit down and watch your dog for a while. Make a habit of it. You will note that sometimes he carries both ears very erect and forward. Sometimes one ear is forward and one back, sometimes both will be back, and so on, according to what is happening around him. This in itself can reveal many things to you as the handler.

The dog utilizes his ears as a directional antenna system. He focuses towards the sound with each ear and has the ability to sense, localize, and discriminate sound with extreme accuracy. His use of the ears in the same direction shows that he has pinpointed the sound he is after and is paying close attention to that sound. For a dog which has been trained for protection or to seek out criminals, both ears forward is a definite indication that someone or something is out in that direction. Similarly, while the dog may be paying close watch to an apprehended suspect, and one ear keeps moving in another direction, beware. There may be a second suspect in close proximity to you. The dog has six times the hearing capacity of human beings. Utilizing the dog's senses and understanding what his ear position means may prevent the handler from entering into potentially dangerous situations.

The next component of communication is the dog's use of barks, whines, yelps and growls. The actual sound, the position of his jowls, and the stances he assumes when voicing all combine to indicate some form of instinctive message. A steady rhythmic bark may be considered a warning to danger. A bark consisting of two or three sounds and then quiet may be the dog attempting to communicate with someone and then stopping to listen. Deep-throated growls show anger or warning and sometimes fear. High-pitched yelping usually indicates excitement, playfulness or anxiousness. Crying or whining may show injury or pain, concern, loneliness or fear.

Physical posture also plays an important role in the animal's communication. A submissive animal will cower, ears back, tail between its legs. A dominant dog will hold his tail high above his back, and carry his ears forward and erect; his hackles may go up and the forehead may furrow. The handler can read the degree of aggression on the part of his partner by watching how far the lips are retracted from the gums, and how intense the dog appears from his forward ears, hackles, and type of bark.

The animal's tail, when over his back, shows complete domination. When it is held halfway out from the body this is a ready or danger signal. A tail which is held down shows a non-aggressive or relaxed state, whereas the tail held down between the legs expresses fear.

All of these components may appear at some time in different combinations. For example, a very dangerous and unpredictable dog is the fear biter. He shows aggression, hackles up, feet firmly placed, steady snarl or bark, and the tail out from the body. The indication that he is a fear biter is the position of his ears, held back against his neck. They are not forward,

as they would be in an aggressive, confident police or protection dog who otherwise shows the same physical signs during the threat or attack stage.

Take the time to sit back and watch your dog and to learn his ways of reacting to different situations. Study him carefully and observe his body language. In training and on the street, that body language is going to be how he communicates to you. He reacts instinctively and does not intentionally communicate with you all the time. Therefore it is up to you to learn his little idiosyncracies and to pay close attention to what your partner is saying. Soon it will seem that his body language is screaming out messages to you of which you were previously unaware. On the street, those messages may just save your life.

K9 officers are involved in more shootings than any other division of law enforcement. At most American police K9 seminars, fully fifty to sixty per cent of officers in attendance have been involved in gun battles with encountered suspects. Don't take your partner's natural attributes lightly — take advantage of them.

One last word on communication between you and your partner. You will find that your dog will start to automatically cue to certain actions on your part. For example, every time you pick up the car keys, he gets excited because you're going for a drive, or he gets excited as you are preparing to go for a jog or putting your uniform on for work. Dogs learn to read our body language and actions just as we learn to read theirs. This should be remembered at the start of training. Each time you do an exercise it should be done exactly the same way. For example, every time you command *heel* always start on your left foot. Everytime you command *stay* start on your right foot. Soon your partner will cue in automatically without being given a verbal command. Remember, whether you realize it or not, communication is going both ways.

Telegraphing

Telegraphing occurs when you as the handler indicate by some subtle movement that something is about to occur. You must train yourself not to make accidental signals which may confuse the dog, for this could set back your training drastically. It may appear that it is your dog that is failing, while in fact you are probably reinforcing the problem by unwittingly telegraphing things to your dog.

The example of a dog I trained explains this. During its young life this dog had a bad experience with a car and his fear of traffic was intense. I would take him onto a local city traffic island and heel up and down as traffic passed by. Each time a vehicle approached from behind, the dog would break heel and force his way to the centre of the island, nearly always forcing me over with him. I would vigorously correct him with the lead but could not break him of his fear until I realized what I was doing. Every time I heard a vehicle approaching from behind I would carefully brace up on the lead to prepare for my partner to bolt. All I was doing was telegraphing to him that I was tensing up as he was hearing the offending vehicle approach. He could have had no way of knowing that I was tensing up because of his anticipated reaction, and not because I too was afraid. Once I learned to cease telegraphing to my dog and enforcing his fears, I was able to take him into traffic, and with patient perseverence and controlled corrections, successfully built his confidence in high-traffic areas.

Keep this in mind in all aspects of your training. Whether or not you know it, your dog is always aware of your slightest changes from the norm. Be it something as subtle as a change in your pace of breathing, in your body tension, or in the way you hold the leash, he is conscious of it, and it will affect the way he acts or reacts in a given situation.

4

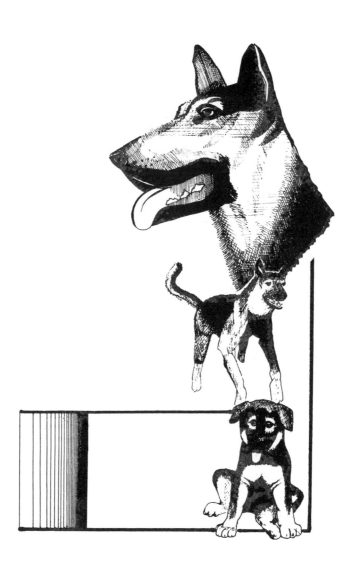

4
Puppy Selection

Most police departments have a tendency to utilize donated dogs when they reach an age of eight to twelve months, mainly due to considerations of budget and manpower. The problem with this method is that the dog's personality, habits and traits have already formed. These can be very difficult, if not impossible, to change. Some of these habits, in fact, may be the reason the owners have donated the dogs. There was some aspect of the dog's behavior which they couldn't change or control, and the department inherits an animal which is potential trouble.

The advantages of the bonding process between dog and handler are also lost, and while there will be bonding, it will not be nearly as strong as when a pup has been with his handler from nine weeks onward.

Although a pup purchased between eight and ten weeks of age has a lot of unknown factors in his makeup, this pup can be raised and developed as a potential police service dog. His personality, habits and abilities can be patterned by his handler and, should any problems arise during his young age, these can be worked on, or the pup can be replaced before much formal training is expended on the animal. Any shortcomings the pup may have will be highly visible during his first eight months. A donated adult dog which doesn't succeed in the formal training is a waste of money and manpower.

Restricted budgets require the best possible chances for success the first time around. Handlers should be chosen who show patience, perseverence, genuine love for the breed, and willingness to dedicate much time to the program. Training does not cease when the team leaves the kennels. It must be constant, and the officer and his family must take the time to show the animal his acceptance as a family member.

When buying a puppy for the home, police or security work, take the time to check into various kennels as well as private breeders. Study the pedigrees to ensure purity and attempt to deal with breeders who will place a guarantee on the pup should elbow or hip dysplasia develop. Reputable breeders will have no hesitation in providing such a guarantee. Purebreds which are registered with the Canadian Kennel Club or the American Kennel Club are preferable but not an absolute must.

Look carefully and get references from people who have bought dogs from the breeder you are considering before making a decision. If possible, look at other dogs sold by the breeder to ensure they are of good temperament. Once you have located a few reputable breeders it is time to choose the puppy you want.

In choosing a puppy, the handler should first watch the pups as a pack and observe each one. The ideal choice is an aggressive, self-confident pup who shows leadership over the others, and who will readily approach you as a stranger without hesitation or fear. Ideally the search is for the Alpha male of the litter, or the next closest prospect, depending on temperament. Those who have an opportunity to see the pups suckling the mother will note that the leaders of the litter will almost always be using the teats nearest the mother's front legs. These teats yield more milk and therefore the dominant pups force the others to less lucrative positions.

Beware of pups that whine, howl or bark constantly when excited as these habits may be hard to break and can be extremely annoying. These pups are very often anxious and although in other tests may rate high, they may have a tendency to be high-strung and are often hard to settle down.

Once you have chosen one or two prospective pups, they should be removed one at a time from the litter to a location totally separate from the mother and other siblings, preferably to a place completely unfamiliar to the pup. This places stress on the puppy, and will test his ability to adjust to his new situations. He should react positively to his new surroundings by investigating where he is and becoming accustomed to his new surroundings. He should also respond to you in a friendly, confident manner without fear or anxiety. If the pup has a favorite toy, play with him for a while, and throw the toy a short distance to see if he will retrieve it for you. It is not necessary that he return the toy, only that he show an awareness of it, that he is playful, and is not afraid to carry something in his mouth.

Now that the puppy is showing some confidence, play and rough-house with him a bit. Ascertain whether he is willing to take a bit of playfulness without shying or running scared. There is no need to be very rough, simply wrestle and tease him enough to get him worked up. Barking or playing along is an excellent response. Take a rag and try to play tug of war with him. Tease him. Again, joining in the game is a good response. At some point squeeze one of his toes just firmly enough to cause him some pain. He should be quick to forgive you and become trusting again.

The next test is again very simple, and enables the handler to test the pup for his reactions to sudden, new and unsettling noises. Take any two metal objects, such as a pair of hubcaps, and bang them together in front of the pup. The noise need not be excessive, only enough for the pup to notice it. If he shies away suddenly and shows some hesitation, this is acceptable, as long as he recovers and does not continue to show fear. The idea is to test the pup's recovery time, to see that he is able to adapt to new sounds and surroundings, and in particular, that he reacts happily and confidently towards you as a stranger.

Older pups, in the six- to eight-month age range, can also be given the gun test. Put the pup on a leash and have a suspect with a revolver containing blank loads suddenly appear and fire a few rounds into the air. The pup may balk a bit, but as long as he doesn't break and try to run or show a lot of fear or anxiety, he should prove satisfactory. In most cases the reaction of a solid pup will be one of curiosity. His ears will perk up and he will show much interest in what is going on. Other candidate pups may even bark or lunge at the suspect, which is an excellent response.

One final test I utilize is with an umbrella. The shape of an umbrella is very strange to some dogs and when opened suddenly, it can provoke unusual reactions in a dog. Stand facing the dog, with the umbrella in the closed position and the top pointing towards the dog. Have the handler place the dog on lead at a sit position. Without warning, open the umbrella with a sudden fluid movement so that the dog is suddenly facing a new, unusual object. The ideal reaction is the same as that in the gun test sequence.

When you have chosen your candidate pup you have made a decision which will alter your daily way of life for years to come. You will have initiated a friendship between you and your new partner which is closer and stronger than any other involving man and animal. Whether you mistreat this dog or treat him royally, you will find him extremely dedicated;

he will worship you for the smallest amount of love and praise which you may offer in return. This degree of blind dedication is but a small indication of how strongly these animals feel about us. Therefore, we must simply return that love and be patient during our training periods, and the dog will do his best to please us.

The key to dog training is simply this: the dog already knows how to jump, run, track, attack and even search for articles. It is all part of his natural instinct. We only have to learn how to persuade him to utilize these abilities for us. We must be willing to learn how to communicate our wishes to the dog, and how to read what he is telling us, both by body language, and by his barks. (These aspects have been dealt with in the section on *Understanding and Reading K9 Behavior.*)

Once you have your puppy at home, prepare an area which is clean and warm, preferably a spot which can be his own, where he can be alone if desired. Dogs, like people, often need time alone so they can relax and unwind without the interference of young children or other distractions.

An adequate supply of food and clean water should be maintained, as well as a supply of dog biscuits. This is an excellent treat and is good for maintaining clean, healthy teeth. Rawhide chewables are also excellent for the puppy, especially through the chewing stages when he loses his baby teeth and the adult teeth start to grow in.

If a pup has one floppy ear, this can often be corrected by feeding him plenty of biscuits and letting him do a lot of chewing. This exercises the supporting muscles which run behind the mandible (jaw) and upwards to the base of the ear, and more often than not will correct ear faults. If the floppy ear persists, see a veterinarian for correction. It is extremely important that the ears be properly erect, as a lot of what the dog tells you is translated from ear carriage and direction.

Although you may do some training with your pup before he is eight months of age, do not expect him to be totally obedient and to understand you fully. He is still a pup, and for him to grow up mentally and physically healthy, he must be allowed to be a puppy through his adolescent and teenage period before he can be expected to act like an adult.

Give your puppy plenty of playtime as well as lots of quiet time alone. Teach your children the importance of leaving the puppy alone and not to be persistent in playing with him if it appears he would rather lie down. In most cases where the dog at home bites a child, the dog is instantly corrected and sometimes even destroyed in the heat of the moment. The handler later learns that the dog had tried repeatedly to avoid the child, and had finally bitten in frustration. This is not to condone the biting, as the dog must be corrected in such instances, but only to emphasize that the children and others living in or visiting the household must be strictly taught to respect the dog's feelings and needs. He too is an individual.

As the pup begins to grow into adulthood he should be taken to the vet to have X-rays taken, to determine any signs of hip or elbow dysplasia. This disease can be very painful to the animal and can cripple him badly. If it is present in the animal, serious consideration should be given to replacing him. The disease usually intensifies with time, disabling the dog so that he will have to be replaced eventually in any case; the heartbreak of watching your partner degenerating to a crippled state is another consideration. To keep these problems to a minimum, any dog which needs to be replaced for medical or other reasons should be detected as early as possible by constant monitoring for any incapabilities and medical problems. (Further details on dysplasia are found in the *Illnesses* section of Chapter 6.)

Pups at eight or nine months of age may become skittish and act differently. This is a stage analagous to human puberty and will eventually pass in many cases. Give the animal a chance to recover, and you will likely find it is a normal part of his growing up.

Some light training may be done prior to the pup reaching six months of age and preferably by eight months. This allows the animal time to mature, and also allows his neck muscles to strengthen so that he is capable of withstanding proper choke chain correction, which is the most important corrective action used during training procedures.

Remember, dog training is no place for tempers. You must always be patient and realize your puppy may not understand what you are trying to do. One loss of temper can set back your training for weeks. If you begin to get frustrated with your puppy, stop, relax and give both yourself and your partner a break. We all have our off days.

5

5
Raising
the Potential
Police Service Dog

Having chosen the puppy, you must raise him in a manner that will prepare him physically, mentally and emotionally for police service work.

First, take the puppy home and introduce him to his new environment. As mentioned in the previous chapter, give him a place where he can go to be alone if he desires. Allow him to explore his new habitat.

You will by now have decided what to feed your puppy, remembering that the nutritional requirements for a puppy will not be the same as those of an adult dog. However, avoid foods which promote rapid puppy development, as these so-called puppy foods promote the pup's growth at such an accelerated rate that the bone structure is not set sufficiently to handle the fast increase in weight. Thus, in some cases, hip dysplasia may occur where otherwise it may have been avoided. Ask your veterinarian for his recommendations.

Once the puppy is settled in, the first and foremost training task is that of housebreaking. The best way I have found to persuade him to do his business where required is simply to make sure he spends a lot of time outside at the same location and on the same schedule every day. Praise him every time he is successful. Put him out immediately after feeding, immediately upon awakening in the morning and after any naps. If you prefer that he uses a particular spot, take him to that area each and every time.

At night, keep him confined to a small area with one side being his sleeping area and the other his training area. If you find your puppy is not succeeding in training, try using a small kennel such as those the airlines use and lock him inside during his sleeping periods. He will not soil or wet his own bedding if he can possibly help it. When he wakens, lift him immediately outside and as soon as he does his business give him lots of praise.

A scolding is in order if he has an accident, but remember he, like any infant, is still learning control, so don't overdo it. Scold just enough to let him know you are disappointed, not angry. It won't be long before you are successful.

Another immediate priority with your new puppy is to help him through his teething stage, usually around ten to twelve weeks of age. Your puppy should be provided with rawhide chewables or even Milkbone to chew. He should also be given a toy which he can play with and chew. These articles will satisfy his need to chew and help prevent destructive chewing on furniture. If you find him chewing on anything other than what is permitted, correct him firmly and immediately. Never correct him unless you catch him in the act, or you will do more harm than good.

Should destructive chewing persist, see your veterinarian and have your puppy's diet checked. He may be suffering from a mineral deficiency, which could even cause the pup to chew at his own coat. Should there be a chance of mineral deficiency, attempt to correct it with organic, rather than chemical, supplements because the organic supplements tend to give better results. My own dog went through this stage and chewed himself raw in spots until his diet was changed and mineral supplements given. I have found that a product called Sulfodene, presently only available in British Columbia and the United States, works well for topically treating these and similar "hot spots."

The most important thing to remember while raising your puppy is to let him be a puppy. Allow him to enjoy his adolescent and teenage periods and do not expect the results you would from an adult dog. This doesn't mean, however, that you can't start training your puppy before he is nine months of age. On the contrary, as you associate with your puppy encourage him to do simple exercises.

Show him how to sit, using the appropriate command, and make a game of it. Every time he wants a treat, make him sit and then reward him with praise and the treat. When you see him starting to lie down, do a bit of word association by commanding *down* as he performs the task. Once he lies down, give him lots of praise. He was going to lie down anyway, of course, but it won't be long before word association with this and other natural movements will begin to mean something to him. In addition to word association, take the time to gently place him in the desired positions and use the appropriate commands. (See Chapter 8 on hand signals.) Don't make a long training session of it; periodically throughout the day, once or twice each time, is sufficient. He will soon catch on, and everything he learns now will make things much easier when we start on his formal training. This time of your puppy's life is very influential in the makeup of his personality and on the way in which he will grow up and socialize. Keep this in mind and mould him into the type of dog you want.

Take a lot of time with your puppy to play games with him. Two very important games which most puppies love are fetching a ball and tug of war.

With regards to fetching, do not expect your puppy to bring the ball back to you right away, as this will come with time. It is usually best that the ball also be his own toy. This way, he becomes attached to it and is more likely to pick it up and carry it back to you. My preference is to use a hard rubber ball. Soft rubber or tennis balls can be chewed up and ingested by your puppy; this is dangerous and potentially life-threatening. A recent example of this type of problem occurred when an officer noticed his K9 partner was vomiting and losing weight. All attempts to cure the animal failed until the veterinary surgeon ordered a series of X-rays, which showed a collapsed tennis ball lodged in the dog's intestine. (Surgery to remove the ball was successful and the animal recovered fully.)

Also, ensure that the ball is not small enough for the dog to choke on. Recently an officer had a bad experience when his partner got hold of a racquetball. It easily slipped into the dog's throat and the animal came very close to choking to death. Fortunately veterinary assistance was close by and the dog's life was saved. Had the problem not been discovered quickly and urgent medical attention given, the incident would most likely have been fatal.

As you throw the ball, use the word *fetch* to associate the command to the game. If he picks up the ball, coax him back to you and associate it with the command *come*. Always make sure the game is fun and never force your puppy or expect him to continue the game once he tires of it. Like any child his attention span may be very short.

For tug of war, take a towel or gunny sack and gently tease the puppy with it until he shows an interest in it. He may not make any attempt to grab it at first, but if enticed carefully, it won't be long before he does. While teasing him with the towel use the words *take him*. Be excited and get him playful so he wants to play the game. If he grabs the towel let him have it and give him lots of praise. Keep at it until over a period of time you can have a good struggle over the towel. When you have him playing well and you want him to learn to let go of the towel, stop struggling, hold the towel firm and still, and sharply use the command *out*. He many continue the game, but don't comply. Command *out* again sharply, and using your forefinger over his nose and placing your thumb in the corner of his mouth between his teeth, gently separate his jaws enough to release the towel. Again repeat the command and when the towel is released, praise the dog.

Remember always to use only one-word commands where possible. In some cases two words are acceptable. Use his name frequently and as a key word for any movement command, in order to draw his attention.

Remember, he is still a puppy. He needs to explore and investigate the things around him. His attention span will be short and he may lose interest in things quickly. Let him enjoy these early parts of his life. Make them fun and you will still be amazed by what he can learn. Keep in mind the bonding process, and make sure you are his best friend.

6

6
K9 Care
and Nutrition

Kennel

Now that you have a K9 partner you must make arrangements to house him adequately. As he is to become a police service dog, or personal protection dog, the animal should be allowed to live as a member of the family. He should be permitted access to the house and given his own sleeping area or, if acceptable, be allowed to sleep wherever he prefers.

In my own case, my partner is given free run of the house during the day, and at night he has chosen to sleep on the floor next to my side of the bed. This freedom allows him to maintain his social position within our household and to go anywhere in the house to be alone and sleep if he desires.

Although this is the ideal arrangement, there may be those who will not be able to have the dog inside at all times. There will also be those who have large families, and the only way your partner will be able to get adequate rest during the day after a particularly stressful nightshift is to have a place of his own, away from other members of the family.

My personal recommendation is a ten-foot by twelve-foot run with a smooth concrete pad for a floor. Metal posts should be placed in the concrete and six-foot chain link used to enclose the kennel. A peaked roof of pressed fiberglass should also be built over the top of the enclosure. This provides shade on hot summer days, as well as protection from precipitation.

A doghouse made of yellow cedar should be provided at one end of the kennel, opposite the side where the kennel gate is. There are two ways to do this. It may simply be placed inside the kennel in a corner, but this takes away some space from your dog inside the enclosure. Preferably, the doghouse is built as an extension to the pad so that it sits outside the enclosure. The dog has direct access to the kennel, as the door of the doghouse is matched and connected to a hole cut in the chain link. The cut portion of the chain link should be framed by two-inch by four-inch board and nailed to the doghouse. This will prevent your K9 from cutting himself on any exposed wire, and will also keep the wire from falling apart or peeling back.

Because dogs have an aversion to chewing yellow cedar, its use in building your doghouse will help prevent chewing problems with your young puppy. The doghouse itself should not be large, as the dog must warm it with his own body heat and will not be able to keep himself comfortable in too large an area. Make it just large enough for him to move into comfortably.

It is not a requirement to have a concrete pad, but I have found I never have to worry about digging by the dog, and all it takes is a quick washdown to clean up. If using a concrete pad it is wise to slope it slightly, away from the direction of the doghouse, to permit water runoff. Sloping the concrete pad will allow your partner to go to high ground and will prevent water from pooling during inclement weather.

Feeding and Nutrition

There are so many dog foods on the market today, each with its own benefits and disadvantages, that it is difficult to decide what to feed your partner.

There are frozen meats, canned food, dry food, as well as the new moist and meaty type of dog food. In choosing, you must find one that is easy and convenient for you to store. The food must contain all the protein, minerals, vitamins, fat and carbohydrates required by the dog, as well as the appropriate amino acids. His food intake should be balanced and should supply him with the amount of energy necessary to do his job. Your veterinarian can assist you in ensuring a proper diet.

The police service dog is under constant stress when working and proper diet is therefore essential to keeping him in top working condition. Avoid giving table scraps, as this may upset the balance of nutrients you have worked so hard to maintain.

While on long tracks, it is wise to carry a small bag of snacks to feed your K9 in order to maintain his energy level and to reward him for a job well done. These snacks should be of the same type as you give him at home.

My own preference is to serve a dry dog food. Wayne pet food products such as Wayne Chunk-size have produced excellent results for me. I store it in a large plastic garbage container which can be sealed shut against moisture. It has high calorie content, is in itself a totally balanced meal, and can be fed dry. Although I feed mine dry, and it is palatable to my partner, some dogs may not find it so appealing, in which case water can be added to make a form of gravy. This food is easily carried in the patrol car, as well as in the pocket for use on extended searches.

There is now on the market a product scientifically produced so that the amount of food given to the dog is reduced by about two-thirds. This decreases the amount of stool excreted by the dog, and makes carrying food easier on long-distance tracks. The product was designed for war dogs during the Vietnam conflict, in order to provide the handlers with food they could carry on long weekly patrols. It nourished the dog adequately while creating minimal weight and bulk. This type of product is still available on the market but is usually a bit more expensive than standard dog foods. (When one considers that it goes much farther than the standard product, however, the difference in cost becomes negligible.) One product which I find reasonable in cost as well as high in quality is the Iams line of dog foods. This product would be particularly beneficial to dogs which endure stressful working conditions.

Under no circumstances would I ever feed bones other than ball joints. Most bone has a tendency to splinter when chewed and may become very dangerous if ingested by your dog. It is far preferable to feed products such as Milkbone which assist in fighting calculus (tartar) and exercise the jaw muscles. Never feed raw eggs to your dog as this causes a biotin breakdown and subsequent digestive problems in the animal.

The feeding bowl should always be kept very clean, with frequent washing to prevent the formation of bacteria and to help maintain your dog's health. Stainless steel bowls are the most durable and easily maintained types of feed bowls and I strongly recommend them over any other style. They also provide a natural deterrent to puppies who like to chew on their feed bowls. Feeding bowls made of plastic occasionally cause allergic reactions around the muzzle of the dog, which is another reason I prefer the stainless steel type.

Always ensure that your dog has an adequate fresh water supply at home and in the police or security patrol car. A non-spill type of water pail can be acquired which consists of a water bucket covered by a deeply grooved cap with the centre removed.

Consult your veterinarian immediately if your dog appears to be having any unusual bowel movements or digestive problems. It may be due to the type of food he is eating and a change may be required. Some dog foods are just too rich for some dogs to handle.

Grooming

Grooming your K9 is essential for various reasons. First, it allows you and your dog a period of time together each day in a totally relaxed atmosphere. During this time your dog is brushed, rubbed, petted — in short, all his dreams come true. (After all, show me a dog who doesn't love to have his neck or tummy scratched for hours on end!) This is an ideal bonding process in itself which the dog will look forward to each day, and which will strengthen your friendship with each other.

Second, it gives you the opportunity to systematically examine every part of your dog for any medical problems. Often you will feel a growth under the dog's coat during grooming, whereas you would never have noticed it otherwise. During a grooming session, for example, I felt a growth on my dog's neck which was virtually invisible. It turned out to be a mastocytoma, a cancerous growth, and was subsequently removed by surgery. He has had no further problems, but the disease could have become more serious had it not been discovered.

Finally, your dog's coat protects him from the cold and the wet, and should be maintained in good condition in order for him to work at peak efficiency. If he is a police service dog he has a public image to uphold as well, and it is important that he always look his best.

For grooming, find a location where you won't be disturbed, and start with your hands at the base of the tail. Using both hands rake your fingers briskly against the natural fall of the hair, massaging the skin as you go. Make sure you cover his entire body thoroughly. Check his anal glands and testicles, and note any problems or malformations. On one of your routine trips to the vet he can show you what to look for. This is the best way to learn what is normal and abnormal on your dog. (I strongly recommend a medical check for your dog at least every six months.)

As you progress you will find hair, both the outer layer and the down-like hair underneath, falling out in clumps and gathering in balls as you massage forward. (The downlike hair is an insulating coat and the outer coat acts as a water repellent.) As you continue forward, check the pads of his feet and his nails for tears or tenderness. Check his ears for blockage or infection. Feel the base of each ear with your palms cupped around them. If one ear is much warmer than the other and he has been shaking his head, scratching, or flicking his ear periodically, it is likely that the warmer ear is infected. Carry on to check his eyes for clarity, discharge or irritation. It should be noted at this point that the dog has three eyelids over each eye — the upper and lower lids and the "third eyelid" known scientifically as *membrana nictitans*. This third eyelid is an opaque membrane located at the inner corner of the eye. The membrane flicks across the eyeball when-ever the cornea is touched, threatened, or when pressure is applied to the eye. Its purpose is to clear out any dirt, dust, or insects and to moisten the eye surface with tears. Any excessive tearing or mucous discharge from the inner corner of the eye should be watched carefully to prevent infection. Should you detect a problem or any unusual or sudden change in the eye, seek immediate medical advice.

For the dog to scent properly he must have moist lining in his nasal passages. If the nose is dry it may be due to dehydration or illness. Ensure that he has adequate liquids and if the problem persists, again seek assist-ance from your veterinarian.

Now check the teeth to make sure they are not broken and that no foreign substances have become lodged between the teeth. Check the gums for firmness and color. Check the vomeronasal gland behind the upper

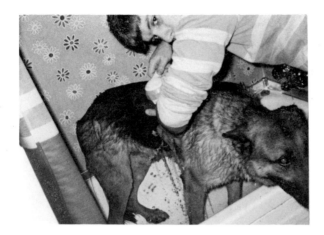

canine teeth to ensure there is no swelling or injury. (For further information regarding the vomeronasal gland see Chapter 9 under the heading *Tasted Scent*.)

Once you have loosened and massaged his coat fully, take a soft brush and thoroughly brush the hair going first against, and then with, the lay of the hair. This will remove the loose hair and dead skin you have loosened during the massage.

Under no circumstances should a wire brush be used, as these have a tendency to scratch the skin and remove hair from the follicles before it is ready to fall. This may cause the dog some irritation. All the hair that is actually loose will be removed by the hand massage and soft brushing alone.

A properly-groomed dog seldom needs bathing. The natural oils which coat his skin and fur are removed during bathing and take two to three days to be replaced. When you do bathe your dog, ensure that no water gets into the ear canals, and avoid soap around the eyes. Use only a mild pet shampoo, and make sure he is adequately dried before going outside on cool days to prevent the possibility of him catching cold. Again, avoid bathing him too often as this interferes with the natural oils in his coat and may cause irritation.

Inoculations

Inoculations should be given at six weeks of age and again at twelve and sixteen weeks. These inoculations should include distemper-hepatitis, leptspirosis, parainfluenza and canine parvovirus. Rabies vaccine and annual booster shots should also be administered according to your veterinarian's recommendations.

Veteri-narian	HUFF ANIMAL HOSPITAL
Address	1512 56th St.,
City Province	Delta, V4L 2A8

VACCINATION CERTIFICATE

OWNED BY	
ADDRESS	
CITY PROVINCE	

Date: Oct 18/84

CERTIFICATE OF VACCINATION

This is to certify that on this date I have vaccinated the animal described below against:

Pet's Name _____ Klause _____ N. Sex _____

Color & Markings _____ Black & Tan _____

Breed _____ G. Shep _____ Age _____ 7 yrs. _____ Weight _____

Rabies Tag No. _____   Vaccine Serial No. _____

Veterinarian _____

CLIENT COPY

CANINE
- ☒ Distemper
- ☐ Distemper/Measles
- ☒ Lepto C-I
- ☒ Parvo
- ☒ Hepatitis (CAV-2)
- ☒ Parainfluenza
- ☐ Bordetella
- ☐ **RABIES**

FELINE
- ☐ Panleukopenia
- ☐ F. Rhinotracheitis
- ☐ Calicivirus
- ☐ **OTHER**

Illnesses

There are many symptoms of illness in the dog which you should watch for. Constipation or diarrhea are common problems and may be due to improper diet or, in the case of diarrhea, worms. If your dog seems to have a voracious appetite, this may be a symptom of tapeworms. A loss of appetite also may indicate worms or stomach disorders. Stomach upsets are often associated with chills, and veterinary attention is recommended.

A hot, dry nose may indicate a fever in the animal, as will excessive water intake. Monitor these symptoms closely and seek assistance if they persist.

If you change your dog's diet, diarrhea may result and should disappear with time. If diarrhea occurs, monitor your dog's intake of liquids to ensure that he does not become dehydrated. Simple treatments of uncomplicated problems such as diarrhea or constipation (which are caused by unclean utensils or diet changes) are the use of common human remedies such as Kaopectate or castor oil respectively.

The most important all-round first aid treatment for a dog which is vomiting or has diarrhea is simply to withhold food for at least 24 hours. Water may be given frequently in small amounts.

Parasites

Parasites may be internal or external. Some of the external parasites carry other parasites which may be transmitted to the dog internally. For example, mosquitoes and fleas can infect the dog with internal parasites.

To determine internal infestation, regular fecal samples should be taken to your animal clinic for microscopic examination. If there are parasites present they can be properly identified and the appropriate medications prescribed.

Kennel Cough

Kennel cough is a dry raspy cough which is very stressful and highly contagious. It is caused by a virus, and medical assistance should be acquired immediately. Separate the infected animal from other K9 members of the unit and from family pets. Disinfect his kennel and all the vehicles he has been in, and burn any bedding he may have used. This is necessary to prevent the spread of the disease to healthy animals.

Dysplasia

Hip and elbow dysplasia is a degenerative bone disease prevalent in the larger breeds. It is rated in degrees of seriousness from one to four, with class four being the worst condition. Your K9 should have his hips and elbows X-rayed once he reaches the age of twelve months to check for this disease. Any animal found to have greater than a grade-one case should be replaced immediately, as the disease is likely to deteriorate quickly in the working dog. Overlooking the situation will only bring increased costs and unnecessary problems later on. There is no guarantee as to how long a dysplastic animal will be capable of working, but you can be assured that the disease will worsen faster and is very painful as it cripples an active working dog. Should it be discovered later in his life and cause him some pain or discomfort, the problem can be dealt with surgically, although it is expensive and not always successful.

Polydipsia

This disease is believed to be associated with psychological upset in the dog and may be a sign of advanced stress or anxiety. The symptoms include excessive thirst where the dog may drink from any source, including his own urine. He will also urinate far more frequently than normal, perhaps to the point of dangerous dehydration, if his water intake is being restricted in an effort to treat the problem. See your veterinarian.

Parvovirus

Parvovirus is an ailment particularly dangerous to young dogs. Untreated, it can cause death very quickly. Symptoms include loss of appetite, dehydration, vomiting, diarrhea and profound lethargy. Inoculations for this disease are recommended. Treatment entails intravenous fluid drip and veterinary supervision.

Impacted Anal Glands

The anal glands are located at the rectal opening and often become clogged and inflamed. Symptoms may include a foul odor from the dog, or indications of itching such as the animal dragging himself along the ground in an effort to relieve the discomfort. Treatment by squeezing the glands to evacuate the matter within will usually successfully relieve the problem.

First Aid

First aid for your dog follows more or less the same principles as that for people, with some adjustment being necessary for anatomical differences. Pay particular attention for shock in your dog. Because he does not understand what is happening, extra effort must be taken to keep him calm and relaxed. If he is in pain and excitable, it may be wise to muzzle him before attempting to treat him, as he may misunderstand your intentions and strike out at you in fear or frustration, even though you have been together for many years.

Heat Stroke

This is a very common problem with working dogs, particularly in the summer months. Simply stated, the dog overheats, and in a few short moments can lose consciousness, slip into convulsions and die. Thousands of dogs die each year when their owners leave them in vehicles and fail to leave windows partially open for ventilation. This does not always occur on extremely hot days. Even on relatively moderate days a vehicle left in direct sunlight can heat up dangerously, the glass in the vehicle creating a greenhouse effect and the temperature within rising dramatically in a very short time. The best way to prevent this potential hazard is to seek shade in which to park, leave windows rolled open for ventilation and maintain a fresh water supply in the vehicle. Tinted glass provides excellent protection as well, particularly the silver or gold foil type which reflects the sunlight.

Should your dog suffer heat stroke from overwork or from being locked in a vehicle, immediate action is essential. You must lower the animal's body temperature as quickly as possible. Locate the nearest source of cold running water and soak the dog. If possible, get him into fresh air and shade, and keep pouring the water to him. The convulsions will stop and he will regain consciousness. He will suffer no side effects, but some rest and a trip to the vet for a routine checkup is recommended.

Working dogs may be even more susceptible to this illness than others, as they are constantly in the car, and exercise strenuously while on calls. Monitor your partner carefully and think about the dangers of heat stroke every time you leave your K9 in the car on warm days.

Porcupine Quills

Your dog may encounter the unfortunate situation of meeting a porcupine in the bush, and the resulting injuries can be extremely painful. These quills will have a tendency to work themselves deeper into the dog as time progresses. If unable to take the dog to a veterinarian you may find it necessary to remove the quills with a pair of pliers. I would strongly recommend muzzling your partner where possible. A liberal application of vinegar-soaked gauze near the base of the quills can assist in loosening the skin and softening the quills to ease their removal. Use the pliers at the base of the quill as close as possible to the point of entry, and remove it by rotating the pliers, twisting the quill out. Treat the wounds to prevent infection and take him to the veterinarian as soon as possible. Quills encountered in the dog's mouth, eyes or other sensitive areas should not be removed in the field. Where possible, immobilize the animal and transfer him to the animal clinic at once.

Injured Pads

Pads on the feet of the canine are very susceptible to injury because of the nature of the work involved. On hot summer days running on asphalt for only a short distance can badly blister the pads, producing a very painful lameness. Close examination will reveal that one layer of skin is worn completely off. The larger pads especially are susceptible to damage.

A tear or cut in the pad can also be very painful. Although these injuries bleed profusely and the dog is very tenderfooted, the wounds are usually superficial. Treatment consists of applying antiseptic to prevent infection, bandaging the foot to keep the wound clean if necessary, and giving the dog extensive rest until the injury is fully healed.

I find that wrapping the foot in a Telfa pad and bandaging with a cling material keeps the wound adequately padded, and the dressings do not stick to the wound. A leather bootie is also available which can be placed on the animal's foot to prevent him from pulling at the dressing. It also adds padding, which relieves some tenderness as he attempts to walk on the injury.

Hot Spots

Hot spots are raw sores which are usually irritated by your dog's attempts to lick and clean the wound. They may start as an itch from a flea or tick bite, as eczema, or by irritation caused by hot weather, coat changes, or lack of oils in the dog's skin. Long periods of boredom or a lack of minerals in the dog's diet may also bring on the reaction of chewing a particular area of the skin. Proper exercise, topical treatment of the raw area and a change of diet (including added unsaturated vegetable oils) will help to clear up a problem caused by diet, boredom or weather. A bath with insecticidal soap, and subsequent topical treatments of the injured areas with solutions such as Sulfodene, are applicable to problems arising from flea or tick bites. Consult your veterinarian should the problem persist. Cortisone injections followed up with a prescription of Prednisone tablets may be required for treatment of chronic conditions.

Poisons

There are many poisons with which your dog may come into contact, and most of the remedies used for people will also be effective for your dog. Know the number of your local poison control centre and use it in an emergency. Anytime you suspect your dog has been poisoned and you are unsure of the substance involved, make an effort to obtain a sample to take to the animal clinic for analysis. A universal remedy for cases of poisoning in which you do not wish to induce vomiting is to administer activated charcoal-filled gelatin tablets. The charcoal acts as a sponge, soaking up the contents of the stomach and passing through the digestive system. Syrup of Ipecac or hydrogen peroxide can be administered as an emetic to induce vomiting. Apomorphine, administered by placing a tablet under one of the dog's lower eyelids to dissolve, is the prescribed emetic which I recommend. In all cases be sure to call a veterinarian regardless of whether you feel you have been successful in your treatment.

Shock

Any traumatic injury to your dog, whether internal or external, always brings the possibility of shock. He will become shaky, even unable to stand. His gums will fade from a bright pinkish color to a greyish white as the blood rushes to the vital organs. In all cases keep the dog warm and reassure him. Try to alleviate any pain, and to reduce surrounding activity as much as possible. The idea is to keep him warm, stay by his side to give him reassurance and to keep him as still and as quiet as possible. Shock can kill quickly, so respond accordingly.

Conclusion

This chapter has covered some of the medical and first aid problems you may encounter. It includes only those problems which are very common, and is far from complete. I strongly recommend that you take your partner to the veterinarian on a regular basis as a preventative measure and as a learning opportunity. When making a trip to the vet, I make a point of inquiring about problems I have seen or heard about. I have also spent a fair number of hours studying and learning about medical problems to which the canine is prone. Take the time to learn as much about first aid for your dog as you can.

Watch your partner for any unusual activities or signs, as they may indicate a medical problem. Any noted physiological changes should be seen to as soon as possible by your veterinarian to prevent any possibility of illnesses reaching advanced stages.

I also recommend the use of a K9 first aid kit, supplemented by substantial training from your veterinarian, for those in the field of law enforcement. This will be discussed in detail in the next chapter.

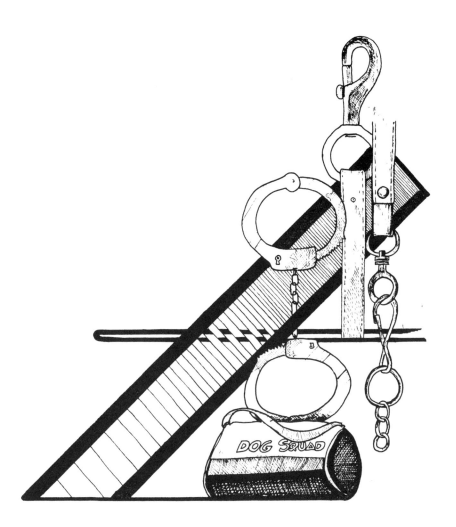

7
Equipment

The dog car, whether for police or security use, should be designed specifically for the use of the K9.

The compartment utilized by the dog should be constructed in a manner which both allows the animal comfort and ventilation and will prevent him from being injured. He should be able to see out the windows while lying on the floor of his compartment.

In a standard four-door car, the rear seat should be removed and a platform covered with rubber matting secured to the car floor. The matting is designed to give the dog traction and provides ease in keeping the vehicle clean. The doors and area where the seat backing was secured should be covered with stainless steel sheet metal, moulded to the shape of the doors and rivetted securely. All sharp edges should be covered with corner moulding. (Moulded plastic or carefully-constructed wood covering can also be used if budget restrictions make this necessary. Stainless steel is suggested to facilitate cleaning.)

If a raised platform is necessary, a floor can be built of plywood and hinged so that it can be lifted up to clean the area underneath. Rubber matting should be glued directly to the floor to ensure stability for the dog.

When in the down position, the floor should be locked securely in place, but latches should not be placed where the dog may injure himself on them. Holes may be drilled in the car floor for ease of washing and draining the interior. These should be two to three inches in diameter, with a proper sealing plug and plug receptacle installed. This will ensure that no exhaust gases will enter the car. In vehicles where no raised floor is required, simply install the base platform directly on the car floor and the rear doors can be opened for easy washing. No drainage holes are required in this type of installation.

The exhaust system should be checked thoroughly and the tail pipes extended just beyond the rear bumper. When alterations are completed, the compartment should be thoroughly checked for any openings which might allow fumes to enter. An easy way to test for leaks is to take the car for a long drive on a dusty gravel or dirt road. Check the car and note where dust has seeped into the compartment. This will identify any leaks. These should be attended to and sealed before the car goes out on the road for active duty.

If permitted by law, the catalytic converters should be removed from the car as well, as the smallest trace of fumes from these converters temporarily diminishes the dog's olfactory capabilities. In some cases, if the animal has had a sizeable dose of fumes from unleaded fuel via the converter, his nose can be temporarily rendered totally inoperable. On an emergency call it doesn't look very good if your robbery suspect just left the scene and you have to wait for your partner's nose to start working again. Where it is impractical to remove the converters, consideration should be given to purchasing vehicles which are not equipped with this device.

Rear windows should be tinted to protect the dog from direct sunlight, and a spill-resistant container installed for the dog's drinking water. If possible the car should be air-conditioned. When air conditioning is used and the windows kept rolled up, the atmospheric pressure inside the car stays slightly higher than outside and prevents fumes from entering the vehicle.

A separator should be installed between the front and rear compartments to protect both dog and handler. Many departments utilize plexiglass with a sliding window. My preference is a steel wire mesh separator with a sliding door. I have found that the plexiglass separator, along with the outside car windows, generates a greenhouse effect allowing heat buildup and inhibiting ventilation. Should plexiglass be utilized, make certain that a large number of ventilation holes are drilled into the panes. These holes should match up in both panes while the window is open to ensure maximum air flow. A wire mesh cage allows for good ventilation and permits some of the heat from the rear windows to dissipate to the front of the car.

There should be a sliding door or window in the separator which can be left open for the dog to exit through and assist the dogmaster should he get into a physical confrontation. The location of the opening in the separator is a matter of handler preference. There are advantages and disadvantages to each means of installation.

An opening behind the driver's head allows the handler to send the dog after a suspect by simply leaning forward and permitting the dog to exit through the separator and out the driver's window. This can be done in an emergency without the necessity of the handler leaving the vehicle. This type also affords excellent handler protection from would-be assailants who may attempt to assault the officer while he is still seated in the patrol unit.

The disadvantage of this installation is the problem of having the dog constantly bumping your head and salivating over your shoulder on a hot day. Also, the headrest must be removed from the driver's seat to accommodate the installation, exposing the driver to possible injury in the event of an accident.

Centre and passenger-side installations afford less convenience during an urgent situation, as the handler must exit the patrol car to effectively engage the dog. Centre installations, however, are ideal for cars equipped with bucket seats, and both centre and passenger-side installations allow the dog to lean into the front compartment without interfering with the driver or drooling on his shoulders.

Should you brake suddenly while the screen is open, your dog may sustain substantial injury no matter where the opening is situated. In the centre and passenger-side installations you need not worry about the dog being thrown into the back of your head, as is the possibility with driver-side openings.

The outside driver's door should also be equipped with a strip of non-slip material from which the dog can jump when exiting the police car in an emergency.

Wide-angle outside mirrors should be installed, as the inside rearview mirror becomes useless with the dog constantly standing in the back.

The entire car should be altered so that there is no chance of the dog catching himself on open corners, of his toes getting pinched where the floor meets the walls of the rear compartment, or of any injury occurring while the dog is moving about in the vehicle. The compartment should be large enough to allow the dog plenty of room to move around, yet small enough that he can prop himself into a corner on an emergency run.

Personal Equipment

Uniforms for the dog handler should be chosen for comfort, wearability and practicality, as well as for good looks.

A two-piece S.W.A.T.-type combat uniform seems to be ideal. The separate shirt and pants allow the handler to wear a belt through the belt loops, to which he can secure his gun belt. A one-piece jumpsuit is practical in some training situations but lacks any means for properly securing the gunbelt; this is particularly important in view of the number of obstacles which dog handlers are required to scale and run through on a daily basis. Deep pockets in the pants and shirt can be used for carrying equipment as well as extra dry dog food on extended tracks.

Properly fitted and siliconed combat boots are very comfortable to wear and will keep the feet warm and dry. They are durable and give excellent support in difficult footing situations.

A baseball cap with identification should be issued as well. I find them to be comfortable and handy in bright sunlight.

The uniform itself is comfortable and can be machine-washed. As well, the material used in most utility dress uniforms tends not to collect dog hair as easily as most uniform material.

The pockets should utilize Velcro closures, rather than conventional buttons or snaps, for ease of operation in the field. The uniforms can also be special-ordered with personal specifications built into the separate components. For example, the pockets on the shirt can be made to fit a portable two-way radio, where it can be more easily heard by the wearer than if worn on the belt.

In addition to the conventional police or security equipment issued, I strongly recommend a piece of personal equipment which no dog handler should be without. This is a high-power, rechargeable flashlight. A standard-issue flashlight simply does not have the power required to search properly in dark, heavy bush areas or in large warehouses. When going on a track for an armed suspect who can see you coming, it is imperative that you have the best possible advantage of light control. A beam such as a 35,000-candlepower flashlight, which will brightly illuminate an area 100 yards deep, will certainly give you a greater advantage when searching for suspects, lost children or discarded articles than will a flashlight throwing off a standard thirty-foot beam. The blinding capacity of this high-power rechargeable can also give you a distinct advantage over the suspect. He can see or hear you coming no matter what type of flashlight you use; if possible, you want to be able to see him before you're close enough to engage him in an armed confrontation. This isn't at all possible with a standard flashlight.

K9 Equipment Pack

Your equipment pack should be designed for easy use, and should carry everything you might ever require. If you need to respond to a callout in the middle of the night, you will never have to be running around looking for your gear. My K9 pack is a large-size gym bag with a separate zippered compartment for raingear.

Inside the pack, articles such as tracking lines, harness, collars, and leashes are each stored in separate leather zipped bags, similar to a shaving kit or travel bag. This is simply for clean and easy storage. When I arrive on a call, I never have to worry about whether my tracking line has unravelled and become tangled with my leashes and other gear. I simply pull out the case required and remove the equipment. It is simple and efficient.

I also carry a roll of white reflective tape in my kit which can be wrapped around the dog's collar or harness. Depending on the situation, this can serve two purposes. First, if working in heavy traffic areas at night, it allows drivers to see the dog should he track out onto the street. Second, should you be working in deep bush and your dog gets away from you in the dark, the reflective tape will easily show you his position with a quick pass of the flashlight.

Maintain your pack by keeping it free of dirt, as it can cause unnecessary wear on your gear. Use proper leather oils to keep your harnesses, collars, and so on soft and pliable.

Should your equipment become wet or soiled on a call, take the first opportunity to empty out the pack, and clean and dry everything. Properly-maintained equipment is necessary for the comfort of your partner and will last you a long time without needing replacement.

K9 First Aid Kit

One of the better seminars I have attended included a course on emergency first aid directed specifically at injuries incurred in the field by the police service dog.

Due to the nature of work involved it is not unlikely that your PSD may suffer traumatic injuries from broken glass or from suspects with knives or crowbars. He may be struck by a passing car or attacked by another dog. He could be injured badly if you are involved in a car accident while on an emergency run, or he may injure himself falling from a high platform. Finally and most feared, you and your partner as a K9 team are more likely to enter into armed confrontations than the members of any other section of the police force. Quick reaction to and treatment of a gunshot wound to your K9 partner can greatly improve his chances of survival.

To this end I recommend a K9 first-aid kit which includes bandages and general first-aid equipment, as well as an assortment of drugs and syringes for injections. I will in no way attempt to explain how to use these items, as you should learn this by "hands-on" instruction from your veterinarian. Keep in mind that this kit should be used only as a last resort as far as drug use is concerned and, if at all possible, the injured animal should be taken directly to your veterinarian for professional assistance. If the animal's injuries are too traumatic to transport him without endangering him further, then the use of this kit should be considered.

ITEMS

1. A watertight steel case, preferably double-latched with the emergency phone number of your animal clinic and poison control centre stencilled on the outside.
2. One roll of plastic bandaging tape, 5 cm x 4 metres.
3. One roll of white tape, approximately 5 cm x 7 metres.
4. One roll of sterile cling gauze, 5 cm x 10 metres.
5. One box of 5 cm x 5 cm Telfa pads.
6. One pen light.
7. One scalpel blade.
8. Plastic bag containing tongue depressors, swabs, gauze pads (6 cm x 6 cm) and cotton balls.
9. Two disposable 3-cc syringes with subcutaneous needles, both capped with *red* sheaths.

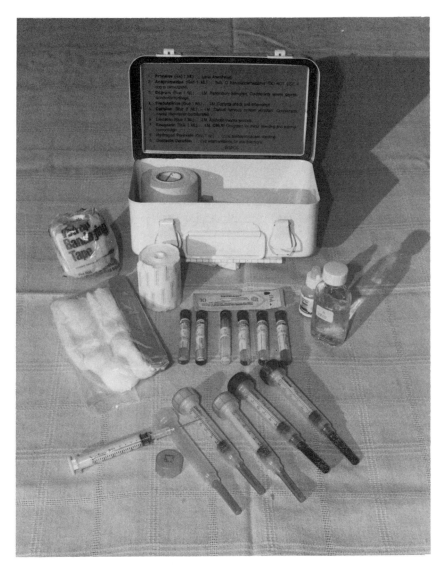

10. Four disposable 3-cc syringes with intramuscular needles, all capped with *blue* sheaths.

11. Seven monoject vials containing the following drugs in quantities pre-measured specifically for the weight of your dog.

    Red Sub Q. A. *Procaine* — local anesthetic
    Red Sub Q. B. *Acepromazine* — Tranquillizer/sedative — *Do not use if dog is convulsant.*
    Blue I.M.   C. *Dopram* — Respiratory stimulant. Counteracts depression/narcotic drugs.

Blue I.M. D. *Prednisilone* — Controls shock and inflammation.

Blue I.M. E. *Caffeine* — Central nervous system stimulant/counteracts depression and barbiturates.

Blue I.M. F. *Lincocin* — Antibiotic/trauma wounds.

Blue I.M. G. *Koagamin* — Coagulant for minor bleeding and internal hemorrhage.

12. Also included should be a small bottle of hydrogen peroxide to be used as an antiseptic or to induce vomiting in the case of poisoning.

13. A vial of antibiotic eyewash for eye infections.

14. A vial or vials of snakebite antivenin for the types of poisonous snakes that are common to the area.

15. For teams working on drug searches, a vial containing the drugs Naline or Narcan for injection to counter the effects of ingested dangerous drugs with which the dog may come into contact.

16. A container of gelatin capsules filled with powdered activated charcoal which can be given orally to the dog to soak up dangerous poisons. This should be used in circumstances where it is not advisable to induce vomiting. It should not be used where a specific antidote is available for the type of poison ingested. This remedy is a universal method of quickly neutralizing the stomach contents. The charcoal soaks up the material and then safely passes through the animal's digestive tract, preventing any of the contents from passing into the bloodstream. Prompt veterinarian assistance is vital in all cases.

17. A small bottle containing tablets of Apomorphine which is the prescribed emetic to induce vomiting when required. These tablets are far easier to use than attempting to give something by mouth. You simply take one tablet and place it under the lower eyelid of the dog and allow it to dissolve. The dog will vomit within minutes. Where Apomorphine is unavailable, syrup of Ipecac can be substituted. Hydrogen peroxide can be used as another alternative. As previously mentioned, veterinary assistance is vital in all cases of poisoning.

A guide which matches the syringe color, drug, vial number and type of injection to be given should be attached to the lid of the first-aid kit. In an emergency this allows the handler to quickly match the right syringe to the proper drug and know which type of injection to give. Again, this training should be given only by your veterinarian and used only if he approves of the emergency procedure. Also take note of the expiry date on your drugs and make sure they are renewed when necessary.

It is recommended that adequate foam padding be utilized to prevent the vials from moving around and breaking. The kit should be firmly secured to the interior of the patrol car trunk where it is out of sight, secure from potential thieves, and removable in case of an emergency in the field.

8

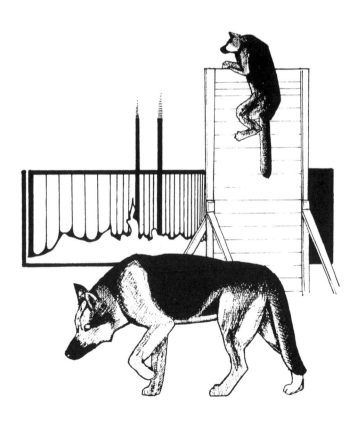

8
Basic
Obedience Training

Before starting, there are a few basic principles which all new dog handlers should know, and which must be adhered to as closely as possible to obtain the desired results. During training procedures (described in this and the following chapters) it is imperative that you concentrate totally on what you and your dog are doing. By now you should know how to read properly your dog's actions and evaluate them, and you should be able to communicate back to him. Now comes the training in which you can utilize your new-found knowledge.

Upon completion of the training chapters you will have a partner that is a pleasure to demonstrate and a pleasure to watch, and a companion in whom you will be able to trust completely.

Training Principles

1. Above all else, have patience. Once again, training is no place for tempers. One bad fit of temper can set training back weeks and does nothing for the relationship between you and your partner.

2. Have a genuine love for and pride in your K9. The animal can sense this and will return that love in effort and companionship. He will do anything to please you. Build on your relationship and bonding by having your dog with you whenever feasible. This will strengthen your relationship, allowing him to understand your actions and behavior as you understand his.

3. Remember, you must communicate with your dog on his level. He does not understand things you say.

4. Never correct or chastise your dog without reason, and then only immediately after a mistake or accident. If the dog seems confused or unsure of what you are trying to do, it is exactly that — he does not understand and does not warrant correction. Only deliberate disobedience should be dealt with from a punishment point of view, and this should be instant correction. Remember, this paragraph is dealing with punishment correction and not training corrections. Most punishment corrections should be nothing more than a scolding. Physical correction such as a slap across the

61

snout or buttocks with the open hand should be reserved for more serious crimes such as chewing furniture.

5. Be prudent and make sure your dog understands exactly what is required of him. Break things down into easier steps if necessary. Once he starts to learn, repetition and praise are the keys to success.

6. Praise instantly a job well done. Encourage and support your dog. Never allow him to injure himself.

7. Training sessions should not be long and tedious. Twenty minutes is plenty of time for the first few sessions. Keep the lessons short and frequent, with much encouragement during each period. Be enthusiastic and this attitude will be reflected by your partner. Make sure to end each session on a good note. If the dog is having trouble near the end of the period, switch to an exercise he knows and performs well. End the session with lots of praise.

8. Do not let mistakes go by. Work on them immediately. A mistake passed by will only cause hours of frustration and extra work.

9. Know clearly what you want to do before your training session begins. If you are unsure of something, don't do it. Get a clear idea of the proper methods before trying them.

10. Make the training period for your dog a fun time of the day. Give him your time, love, patience, praise and understanding and you will soon have a partner to be proud of.

Put an emphasis on control. Polish your dog's behavior. Proper control may save your dog's life, as well as your own.

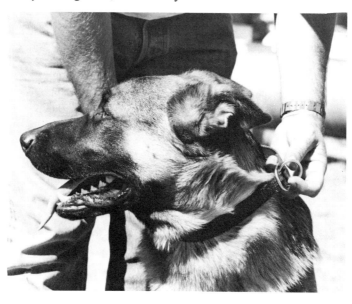

Equipment

Choke Chain

The choke collar is the training collar you will use most. It is the vehicle by which you will correct and control your dog. Do not use pinch collars or leather collars. The use of thick heavy leather collars will come later during the aggression stages of training. The choke collar should be of the large link or nylon variety. It should be sufficiently long to slide comfortably over the head of your dog without forcing it, and yet not so loose that it slides onto his ears if he puts his head down. Neither the large-link collars nor the nylon chokers will wear or damage the hair around the animal's neck, which the standard choke collars have a tendency to do.

Six-foot Lead

The six-foot training leash will be the one required for most training. I prefer nylon leads with quick-release latches. These leashes are sturdy, maintain their appearance and do not stain or rot in inclement weather as do their leather counterparts. Puppies also seem to enjoy chewing on leather items more than nylon, which is another reason I seek good-quality nylon leads. On the average, leather leashes also tend to be more expensive.

Fifteen-foot Longe Line/Thirty-foot Longe Line

The fifteen-foot line will be used for training in obedience and attack work, and the thirty-foot line as a training aid and tracking line. Again, I prefer a strong, flat nylon line in both lengths.

Traffic Lead

A twelve-inch lead with a quick release snap is used for convenience by the officer in the street. It is short and can be clipped to the belt, eliminating the inconvenience of carrying a bulky lead. It also is used to maintain close control of your dog in crowded situations.

These are the only items required to start your dog's obedience training. Equipment for tracking and aggression training will be discussed in the appropriate chapters.

A Word About Corrections

Remember that as your training progresses your pup may attempt to test you to see what he can get away with. If you feel confident in reading your dog's body language, you should be able to tell by now when he is trying to pull a fast one. The trick to successful correction is to catch the fault as soon as the animal is merely thinking of testing the handler. When you are absolutely sure he is about to pull a fast one, give whatever correction is required to solve the problem. Make it a solid correction, and don't be gentle. You need not worry about injuring the animal with choke-chain corrections, and you want to make an indelible impression on your partner so that he no longer even considers intentionally disobeying or testing you. You can't afford to have a dog playing games with you in the field.

If you are working from a distance and he refuses to obey a command, (e.g., sit to a down) and then obeys as you walk towards him, carry through with your correction. Don't change your mind because he went down as you approached. This only shows he is testing your patience to see what he can get away with. Don't accept it. Stick to one command, instant solid correction when required, constant praise for a job well done, and you won't have any problems.

Remember also that your dog does not comprehend what you are saying, and therefore learns his commands only by word association to his actions.

Voice flexation and tone are very important in training. For example, if the dog does something wrong, a firm *no* will suffice. Make sure it sounds like you mean business. Praise should always be given with enthusiasm, and the dog must be readily able to distinguish the differences in your tone of voice.

I have found that most of the dogs I have trained have good memories and learn quickly from repetition. If they are confined in a small room or kennel before and after a training session for an hour or so, they learn their lessons more quickly. This is largely because, beforehand, they become bored and want to come out of the confined area. They will do almost anything just to be released and consequently look forward to the training session as a relief from the boredom of the enclosure.

After the session, when placed back into a small room or his kennel, and not afforded any outside distractions, the animal thinks about what has just occurred. He remembers what he did that obtained praise and he remembers what he did that resulted in correction. While he lies there seemingly at rest, his mind is recalling all these events and is actually reinforcing the instruction given during the lesson.

During the basic training my partner and I went through, he was left in his kennel run all day except for thirty-minute training sessions throughout the day. The results proved to me the success this routine can bring. This method of using a "think-tank" is also excellent after a particularly vital correction which needs to be memorable for the dog. If, for example, you have just had a rather forceful chat with your K9 and physically corrected him for chewing furniture, place him in his place of solitude for three or four hours and ignore him. Ensure that he has no opportunity to become interested in anything by removing all distractions. This isolation, if combined with swift, solid and adequate correction, will straighten up your pup's bad habits much more quickly than if you allow him to do what he wants immediately after the correction.

Heel

I prefer to start active training on dogs between eight and nine months of age, depending on the individual animal. They have matured to the point where they are capable of withstanding proper choke-chain correction, and are very malleable as well. This may not be a desirable age to start working with your dog if he is destined for police work unless you know his ancestral history to be clear of any hip problems. For police service dogs it is preferable to wait until they are twelve months old, so that they may be X-rayed for signs of hip or elbow dysplasia. This decision is based on budget restraints and the cost of starting a new animal into the program should your dog be found to be dysplastic. Barring these problems, training can be successfully accomplished in dogs from eight to eighteen months of age.

Like people, dogs each have individual personalities and learning capabilities. These factors must be taken into consideration and once again, you are the best judge of your partner's ability.

First, place the choke collar on the dog so that when the animal is on your left side, the running portion of the chain goes through the dead ring and over the top of the dog's neck. The ring which pulls the loop of the choke collar closed will be the one which you attach your leash to. Should

you attach your leash to the dead ring your corrections will be useless and confusing to the animal, and will allow the collar to be pulled off if the dog starts to resist.

Now that the leash is applied, hold the line by your left hand with the dog on your left side. Keeping the excess line in your right hand, give the command *heel*, saying your dog's name just prior to the command, and then proceed to walk, stepping out with the left foot.

The reaction you get may be somewhat interesting. Your dog might plant all four feet firmly into the turf, haul back for all he's worth, bolt, fight against the leash, or any combination of these.

Above all, ignore his protests and continue your exercise. When his shoulder is even with you and he is heeling properly, the choke collar should hang loosely around his neck. When at a proper heel your dog should have his right shoulder in line with your left knee.

When he starts to pull ahead, give a short sharp jerk on the leash to pull him in where he is supposed to be. Do the same if he starts to fall back, or if he pulls away. As soon as he is back into position the leash and collar should return to a relaxed state. He will soon realize that he can avoid the correction by staying in position. Don't make any attempts to coax or coddle the dog. Just walk and dish out the appropriate corrections as required.

If you find he is learning to heel well but he still has a tendency to pull ahead a bit, causing tension on the line, use your excess line and in a large sweep, using your right hand, twirl the line swiftly in front of the dog's nose as you walk along. Should he move too far forward the line will come down across his snout and give him a good sharp smack. It won't be long before he learns to stay in position to avoid any corrections.

If the dog bites at the leash or nips at your legs, give sudden instant correction, using a quick snap on the leash or slap across the snout using the command *no*. I do not condone a lot of correction by slapping the dog across the snout, but in some circumstances it is beneficial and can stop problems before they escalate. Never strike the animal on the soft tissue of his nose, or use a solid article on his snout. An open hand is quite adequate. Correction properly delivered in the beginning will prevent prolonged and unnecessary correction in the future which could lead to the dog being "hand-shy."

Do not continue to command the dog once you have started the exercise. Give only one voice command. This will encourage your dog to respond to the one command, and not to wait for the second or third.

When you stop walking simply give the leash a short jerk and praise your dog when he stops. Make sure he doesn't swing his back end away from you or start to pull at the lead.

If he doesn't stand properly beside you, reach down and pull his hindquarters around into position. Demand precision work from your partner. If he pulls away from you, give him a solid choke chain correction and place him into position.

The first few sessions should be short so that the dog can remember what he has learned. Also, two or three lessons a day are ideal at first. Once he starts to catch on, the frequency and duration of the training sessions can be increased.

Give your partner lots of encouragement. Whenever he does an exercise correctly, praise him. You will find him more anxious to please you as time goes on and as he becomes more confident in his abilities.

To implement turns into the heel, start out walking straight ahead, give him the command *heel* again, and make a sharp left turn, walking straight into the dog. He will be forced to reposition himself to prevent being run over. Soon he will be paying close attention to your every move so that he can get out of your way and turn with you. This is precisely the desired result. When he seems confident, drop the use of the heel command prior to your turns and continue this training until your dog is paying close attention to your actions. Soon he will be turning quickly and sharply. For the right hand turns, simply turn right and snap the leash hard to bring the dog into heel. This method can also be used for the inattentive dog who continues to walk ahead of the handler, oblivious to his position. As the dog forges forward, without giving him any word of warning, turn right, even as far as 180 degrees. Utilizing your fifteen-foot longe, allow him a bit of line, take a good solid grip on the leash and while still walking in the opposite direction, snap it up quickly enough to yank the dog out of his tracks. Continue pulling on the line until he is back into position beside you. Two or three corrections of this nature should teach your partner to stick to you no matter what you do. Repeat these exercises continually until he is heeling freely without correction and he shows confidence in his actions.

Once he is confident, distractions should be implemented into the sessions. Children playing with a ball nearby, other pets, livestock, his favorite toy lying nearby, almost anything can be used. He is run through his paces over and over again with sharp corrections given if he becomes distracted and begins to get sloppy. He should be allowed to pay a certain amount of attention to the distractions, but he must also retain his concentration upon you.

An exercise I frequently use is to have one dog walk over the back of another dog which is lying in the down position. This tests both animals' self-control and attentiveness to commands. Continue the exercises until you are satisfied he knows what he is doing and, although he will observe distractions, will make no effort to break away from his heeling.

Take note that your walking pace must be brisk while teaching the dog to heel, as the animal's natural pace is quite quick due to his anatomical makeup. Should your step be shallow and slow, this will be an unnatural pace for the dog and you will be causing him unnecessary difficulty. If you find him having problems try lengthening and/or quickening your step. This move, although simple, can make things much easier and more natural for your partner.

Sit

The next fundamental step in training is the *sit*. Be sure to continue to show your partner exactly what is required of him.

Starting out at heel, walk forward and stop. Give the dog's name followed by the command *sit*. Utilizing the leash in the right hand, lift upwards on the lead and at the same time using your left hand on the animal's hindquarters, press down firmly, encouraging him to sit. Do not turn your body towards him while showing him what you want, as this will indicate to him he is out of proper position. Maintain your original position.

If he sits, give him instant praise. You will find that he may sit and then stand immediately, before his hind end is fully down. If he does, give him a firm *no* as he stands and push his hind end down again. Place him exactly where you want him to be every time. Each time you are successful in getting him to sit, give him praise as soon as his hind end is on the ground. He will soon learn what is desired.

When you perceive that he is beginning to understand what you want, utilize sharp choke-chain correction in a straight upward motion to encourage immediate action on command.

When the dog sits during the first lessons, do not expect him to stay in that position for more than a few seconds, but make certain you get his hind end right down long enough for you to praise him. Don't praise him enough to get him excited, just enough that he knows he has done the movement correctly. If he sits for three or four seconds and then stands, that is fine, as long as he sits fully and can associate the command with the movement. He may seem confused at first, but this is normal. Work hard to help him understand what you want by guiding him into position correctly. *Remember, praise builds confidence.*

Your dog may be a crooked sitter. He may insist on leaning his right shoulder on your left leg or his hind end may be positioned so that he sits

at a forty-five degree angle to you. One reason for the angle problem may be that your body position changes when you are forcing his hind end down into position. Stand firm, and utilizing tension on the leash with your right hand to maintain his head position, place your left hand on his hind end by placing the four fingers on the outside of the dog and your thumb to the inside, and push him into the sit position. This will help to maintain your position and give accurate guidance to the dog.

If he has a tendency to lean against you, simply drop your knee hard and jab him in the shoulder, without saying a word. He will learn to avoid the discomfort by sitting properly on his own.

Continue to position him every time. Demand excellence and precision work. When you find that he starts to anticipate your commands, that is the clue that he knows what is desired. Give him a few more lessons to build confidence, and then revert to only one command and instant choke-chain correction. Give him one command only; if he hesitates give an instant upward correction on the leash, and don't be lenient. A light correction is an invitation to further problems.

When the dog sits immediately on command, give instant praise. Let him know you are pleased with him.

This exercise should continue, combined with the heel, inside and outside turns. Every time you stop, command him to sit.

As before, continue the exercise until he begins to anticipate the command. This is your cue that he knows he is to sit every time you stop. Eliminate the voice command and utilize only the choke chain correction when you stop. This will encourage him to sit automatically, which is the desired result.

During each phase of the exercise you will find that the length of time he stays in the sitting position will increase. This should be worked on in the same manner as when we first had him sitting. Once he is confident, make him stay in the sitting position until you start to walk again. If he attempts to stand, give him a firm *no* and a swift correction with the choke chain, forcing him to sit again. Introduce distractions and continue the training until nothing diverts his attention from you and he can perform all his movements with precision. Always maintain his proper position, reaching down to move his hindquarters when necessary. Don't allow him to be sloppy on even one occasion — accept only perfect performance.

The heel from recall will be instructed near the end of the module which teaches the command *come*.

Down

This command will be a new and unusual position for your dog and there will be understandable confusion at first. Some handlers prefer to take their dogs from a standing position and teach them to down. I have had greater success instructing my dog to down from the sit position, until he learns what is required.

The natural advantage to this method of instruction is that he already has his hind end on the ground, and the trick to putting your partner down is to get both ends to go down at the same time. (That shouldn't be so difficult, now should it?) Many dogs will naturally fight your promptings, more out of confusion than out of intentional disobedience, and if he doesn't want to go down he will simply brace his legs and dig in. For this reason we will start from the sit position.

Once into the sit position, kneel down next to your dog, placing your left elbow over his back with your left forearm running over the back of the dog's neck, and with your left hand grab hold of the lead near the choke chain ring. This will give you control and enable you to balance sufficiently to set your dog off-balance if necessary. Now grasp his left front leg with your right palm on the back of his leg, thumb down, your elbow tucked in toward you, holding him just below the left knee joint. Your right arm should run directly behind the right front knee of the dog. Now give him the command *down*. At the same time gently lean on his shoulders, and pull his front feet forward so he drops into a down position. Don't forget to cue him by using his name prior to giving him the command.

He may struggle or attempt to stand up using his hind end. If he does, lean into him and tug on the choke collar. This will keep him off-balance and will allow you to maintain his down position. As soon as he is successfully down, give him praise.

Each time you perform this exercise allow him an opportunity to move before grasping his leg, as it will be difficult for him to move his leg forward into a down position while you are holding onto it, and he will tend to wait for you to put him down rather than attempting to go down on his own.

Repeat the exercise until he begins to cue to the command. Give him praise and support, continuing the exercise until he is confident in the maneuver. Once he seems to know what is happening, repeat the procedure from the standing position.

If you find that your dog continues to fight your prompting and sticks his hind end up in the air, bring him into heel and once stopped, run the lead under the arch of your left foot, holding the end firmly in your right hand. Give the down command and at the same time force your dog down by stepping down on the lead and pulling up on the slack, using your foot as a pivot point. This procedure can be used with a stubborn partner who refuses to cooperate after he has shown that he understands what is going on. Hold your foot to the ground, if possible directly next to the ring on the choke chain where the lead is attached. Give the down command at the same time and hold firm. This will force the animal's neck down to the ground, and should he keep his back end up in the air, he will soon tire out and relax, eventually lying down in the desired position. Always ensure you can maintain maximum balance and control so that no matter how much he struggles he will never set you off-balance. Only one success for him means extra days of work for you. Remember to praise your dog as soon as he has relaxed into the down position, even though you have had to resort to this forced method of downing him.

If your partner remains stubborn with his neck to the ground but his hind quarters standing up, he can also be prompted by pressing down on the hips. Read your dog as you go along. If he seems confused, go back to the first steps again. Don't forget to use the proper command each time you do a movement, using his name to cue him. Offer him praise immediately as soon as he relaxes into the desired position.

Extend this training until he will go down for you instantly on command from either position. Once you are satisfied he is doing the job well, implement the down-stay and walk away a few steps. Walk back to your dog and praise him for a job well done. Continue his training until all aspects of what he has been taught thus far are done flawlessly. Increase the time he is required to stay in the down-stay position and follow the procedures as outlined in the *stay* module.

There are two problems you might encounter. One is anticipation of the command, with the dog going down before you give him any instruction to do so. The solution is to simply return him to his previous sitting or standing position utilizing a solid choke chain correction. To help circumvent this problem, it is always a good idea to continually change your training pattern so he can never be sure when the commands will come or what they will be.

Another difficulty you may have is that of the dog that will go down when told, but takes his own sweet time getting there. Grasp the lead firmly in both hands next to the choke chain and drive down swift and hard, utilizing all your weight. You will not injure the dog in doing this, so make the correction severe enough that he won't want to experience it again. Utilize this correction every time the problem occurs, and it will soon disappear.

When you have successfully completed the training for the down command, instruct him to sit from the down position. This is opposite to what you have taught him and he may exhibit some confusion. To instruct him in this movement use the opposite correction to the down. While standing beside him when he is in the down position, give him his name as a cue, and the command *sit*. Simultaneously snap the lead upwards and force him into a sitting position. Give him lots of repetition from one to the other and back again until he moves into each desired position on his own accord when the command is given. This will reinforce his training and help to build his confidence as you praise him for his success.

Stay

This command is the most vital and important obedience movement you can instill in your dog. You must demand instant response from your K9 as this is likely to save his life out on the street. He may be so intent on a track or after a suspect that he is totally oblivious to traffic and constantly in danger of being struck down. You must be able to have him cease his actions immediately and stop dead in his tracks without any hesitation.

You may also be able to recognize when your partner is running headlong into other dangers that he does not see or cannot understand. It is not unheard of for a police service dog to be killed in a fall while jumping off the second storey of a parkade in an attempt to apprehend a suspect who has successfully jumped onto the roof or fire escape of the next building. A K9 officer in an American city recently lost his dog off the third storey of a parkade during a training session. This is no fault of either the officer or the animal, as incidents of this nature are bound to occur without warning, but I hope this stresses the importance of having instant control over your partner in situations where you will have enough time to react.

The stay command at this point must be taught as a sit-stay, but the process for teaching the down-stay and the stay from a full run is largely the same. As you progress in your training, include the stay command as a subsequent training lesson to each movement. Make sure your partner becomes polished on each step before carrying on to the next and remember to always introduce new distractions.

Again, start from a heel, walk along and stop, putting your dog in the sitting position. While holding the end of the leash in your left hand, move your right hand in a motion in front of your dog's face with your palm towards him, and at the same time apply tension to the leash using your left hand. Give the command *stay*. While maintaining this tension and enforcing it with the hand signal take one step forward with your right foot and turn to face your dog, almost in a pivot so that the animal couldn't move forward out of his position if he wanted to. Maintain that tension on the lead so he remains in the sitting position. Once your have completed the movement this far, praise your dog. Let him be rewarded for doing nothing. This is precisely what we want him to learn: every time we say *stay* we don't want him to do anything, and if he is doing some particular activity when the command is given we want him to cease that activity immediately.

The next stage is to step back with your right foot into position beside the dog. Again, repeat the steps. Maintain tension on the lead, place your right hand palm towards your dog in front of his face, and give the command *stay*. Step back into position beside your partner and praise him. After you have completed each movement, remember to release the tension on the lead. If during any of your movements the dog attempts to stand or walk forward, use a sharp upward choke-chain correction to maintain him in the seated position. As soon as your pup starts to comprehend what is happening, start to work the stay into your training routine. When he is maintaining his stay without any efforts to move, go on to the next step. Repeat the same procedure as above, starting out on the right foot again, and taking two or three steps forward before turning to face your dog. Maintain the leash in your left hand. Should your dog make any attempt to move, reciprocate immediately with instant correction and repeat the procedure. The next progression is to add distance by utilizing your fifteen-foot line. Continue the same procedure until you can return to the dog by walking on either side of him, and then introduce new distractions. Demand the same attention as you always do when distractions are introduced, and correct heavily for any indication of a break in stay.

You will sometimes find that no matter what you do, as you increase your distance, your dog will move from his position. As you move towards him to administer the appropriate correction he then re-sits and doesn't move. This is not good enough and don't accept it. If you fail to carry through with your intentions you are doing irreparable damage. By his actions he is only showing you that he knows what is required and is testing you to see what he can get away with. Once he has moved, your action should be instant and swift. Utilizing your lead only, literally drag him back to the exact spot he was originally in. Make your correction solid and extremely uncomfortable, swinging him around into position, and then calmly reinforce your command by simply stating *stay*. Do not make any other verbal corrections. Carry out this exercise every time he breaks, even if he only moves a couple of feet.

Once we have taught the dog the down position the same procedure can be utilized, continually increasing the distance as well as the time your animal is expected to stay in position. Ten minutes is not an unreasonable length of time to expect your dog to stay in position without breaking, even with distractions around him. Work on increasing his time as the training continues.

As in the sit-stay position, your partner may have a tendency to worm his way forward while in the down position, or he may stand and then go down again as you approach. This latter incident proves that he knows what is required but is playing that old testing game again. Heavy correction time! Return him to the exact spot in the same position and reinforce your command. Be swift and solid on the correction.

During the stay command lessons, an interesting distraction is to introduce another dog and handler. Make sure beforehand that the animals are not fighters, as they will come in close contact with one another. Put your dog in the sit-stay or down-stay position. Have the other handler, without his dog, walk over to your animal and walk a close circle around him, or over his back if he is in the down position. Have him drag his feet over your dog's back as he goes over. Now have him return and get his dog. Do the same procedure, having him heel his dog right over your partner's back and circling around him as he sits or lies there. During each phase insist on the same quality of obedience with instant corrections should your partner start to break his position. Work him over and over, gradually increasing the time he is required to stay in position.

Once you and your partner are confident with this movement it is time to go to the next stage. Putting your dog at heel, walk along until you reach a position at which you wish him to stay. Without breaking stride, swing your right hand in front of his face, give a short sharp jerk on the lead and at the same time give the command *stay*. Continue walking forward a few

steps and turn towards the dog. Praise him for success. It does not matter whether he sits automatically as long as he doesn't move from his position. If he makes any indication at all that he is going to move give him a firm *no* and reinforce it by extending your right arm, palm towards the dog, and giving the command *stay.* This is done only until you know the dog realizes what is going on. Then it is time to stop reinforcing your commands and use only instant effective correction.

It sometimes helps if, after you have walked away from your dog and he has remained standing, you give the command to sit, followed by another stay command. This will assist him to understand that what he is doing is correct and helps to reinforce him.

Practice this exercise constantly after every new lesson is learned by the dog. After the down, teach him to stay in that position. After teaching recall, teach him to stay in mid-stride. Introduce new distractions and always emphasize control.

The final stage of the *stay* command is that of off-lead training. The animal is left in the down position while the handler leaves the area, totally out of sight of the dog, but in an area where he can observe the dog's actions. Gradually extend the time you are out of sight of your partner until you are satisfied that even with distractions introduced while you are out of sight, he will not even think of breaking his position without your direct command.

This behavior must be fine-tuned to one-hundred-percent reliability so that you will be able to depend on your dog in times of crisis. This emphasis on control also carries over to other aspects of his training and is the key to his success as a precision working animal.

Come

This will be the easiest movement to train your dog, unless of course you have one of those who has a mind of his own and breaks away at every opportunity. If you have followed the steps up to this point, however, you shouldn't have any difficulty.

For this exercise I prefer to start right off with the fifteen-foot line. This allows some distance between you and the dog. When the animal comes to you over that distance it forms a more indelible idea of what is desired than if he takes only two or three steps, as would be the case with your six-foot lead.

Begin with your regular training exercises and leave the dog at sit-stay. Walk out in front of your dog until you come to the end of the lead, dropping the lead loosely on the ground as you go. Turn and face your partner. Give him his name to cue him, followed by the command *come.* You may find that your dog already knows to come to you because of the way in which you brought him up. This is good, but now we want to reinforce this training and teach him to stop in front of you. As your dog comes toward you, take up the slack in the line until he is standing directly in front of you. Using both hands, give a short jerk upwards on the lead to cue him into a sitting position. This being successfully completed by your partner, praise him.

If on the command *come* your dog does not move, pull sharply on the line toward you. Make sure you snap the lead hard enough to bring him to his feet. Pull the line in as he walks towards you and guide him into position in front of you. Once he is seated, give him his reward.

As in the down command, you may find your partner has a tendency to come when he feels like it, or he will wander a bit enroute. The correction is the same. A heavy solid jerk on the line to maintain his attention and straighten him up should be administered as soon as there is any indication of distraction or intentional sluggishness.

If you are having a problem with obedience, particularly with a dog which won't pay attention to you or which bolts away if distracted, this is the time to introduce your thirty-foot tracking line and your most inviting distraction.

Leave about ten to fifteen feet of slack rolled up in the line on the ground and introduce your distraction. Give the command *come* and watch him go after the distraction, whether it be a ball thrown by a child, or another pet playing nearby. As he starts to chase the distraction grab a good hold on the end of the lead and run in the opposite direction. When he come to the end of the lead he will likely come to the end of his disobedience. Follow through by pulling him into you, giving him a cue to sit, and then praise him. He will soon learn that the praise routine is much more pleasant than the "catch it if I can and get choked out" routine.

Repetition being the key to success, this lesson should be taught until done perfectly every time. Once it is thoroughly polished, we will progress the training of recall one step further.

Recall to Heel

Utilizing the six-foot lead, and with your dog sitting in front of you, run the leash around behind you and grasp the end with your left hand. Grasp the leash close to the choke ring in your right hand, give the command *heel* and take two or three steps forward. Simultaneously pull the dog around behind you and allow him to settle into position beside you. Gradually shorten the distance you step forward until finally you don't move. Give the dog the command *heel* and give him a sharp jerk on the line, following through by pulling him around behind you and into position on your left side. Cue him to sit with an upwards correction when necessary. Your dog will soon learn that *heel* means to move into position on your left side, and to stay there at all times. This can be polished by sidestepping towards the dog as well as away from him, and forcing him to maintain position. Utilizing the choke collar as well as a lead looped over his back and under his tummy near his flanks, you may also gently coax him over into position. Do not expect him to step sideways as this is an unnatural movement and difficult to perform. He need only resettle himself beside you. Use the lead over his hindquarters only as a guide.

Now we can implement the *heel* command after the *come* command to give us the finished recall. Repeat the procedures as instructed. Call the dog to you, have him sit facing you, and then command him to heel around and sit on your left side. This is the finished product.

Now implement all these aspects of training together and repeat all phases of obedience in every conceivable place you can. Introduce new and exciting areas to your dog so he can perform in parks, alleys, exhibition grounds, and busy downtown areas with no danger of becoming distracted or fearful of his surroundings.

Retrieval

Some dogs have a natural aversion to holding things in their mouths. The animal we choose for training must readily take objects into his mouth as a requisite for aggression and other situations such as retrieving a revolver dropped during a firefight (gun battle) or stolen articles thrown into dense bush. He must be able to bring these articles back to the handler without causing them any damage. This aspect of his abilities will be used extensively during his service career and therefore must be learned flawlessly.

As the puppy grows up, you should be playing tug of war with him using a strong towel or sack, as well as throwing a hard rubber ball for him. When the pup was chosen he should have shown a lot of interest in such an article. This makes training at this stage much easier.

If your dog loves to retrieve the ball, his training will be simple. Start with your dog at the sit-stay position next to you. Use a traffic lead to ensure he doesn't move until you send him. Throw the ball, and while it is still moving release your dog and in an excited tone encourage him using the command *fetch*.

Once he picks up the ball give the command *come* and follow through with the recall routine. If he drops the ball chastise him lightly at first with a *no*, then encourage him to pick up the ball again using the fetch command. This should be taught as a very playful game until he understands the meaning of the command. Give lots of praise every time he picks up the ball and carries it.

If your dog refuses to cooperate you may have to resort to force-fetching. This is simply placing the dog in a sit position, putting the ball in his mouth and holding the jaws closed, repeating the command *fetch*. Slowly remove your hands and, if he holds the article, praise him. If his jaws start to relax, tell him *no* and press them closed again, repeating the fetch command. Once he has learned to hold the article, command him to *heel* and walk a short distance with him, praising him when finished. Every time you finish the exercise and take the ball from him use the command *leave*. Repeat these routines until your dog will carry the ball. Make every attempt to turn it into a game for him but make sure he follows the rules. Every time he fetches, he is to return it directly to you and hold onto the article until you command him to leave it.

Leave the ball with him in the car and in the kennel to encourage him to use it as a playtoy, but check that he is not capable of chewing it up or swallowing it. This is why I prefer the hard rubber type of ball.

Once he has learned this lesson, replace the ball with another easy-to-hold object such as a wallet or purse. This will allow you to teach him to pick up a different shape as well as to change the weights of the different objects he retrieves. With the lessons well-learned, it is time to teach him how to pick up a revolver by the grips, a closed jack-knife and a plastic bag full of material without damaging any of the contents. Remember there will be times when you will want him to indicate the article and not pick it up depending on the situation, as with some identification and forensic cases. In such instances you can utilize the *leave* command when he properly indicates the article.

Out in the field the use of your dog to retrieve a firearm should be reserved for emergencies only, and should not be considered if there is any possibility of the weapon discharging. Should he chew any articles while fetching, correct him instantly. A chewed baggie of cocaine or heroin in the field could have a deadly effect on your partner.

Train until you can expect accurate results from your dog every time you send him to retrieve. Better results usually occur if it is a game for the dog rather than a workout. This will set the foundation for aggression, drug detection, and area article searches.

Send Away/Area Searches

The command *go* or *send* is the forebear to searching or sweeping an area from a distance. This enables the handler to send the dog out in any direction to search a specific area.

Remember that your partner always wants to be near you and will not like to go away. For this reason you can use a food reward system for this sequence. If he learns that you are not sending him away as a punishment he will be more receptive to the training. As time goes on, replace the food with his favorite article and the occasional wiener surprise. Eventually eliminate the food enticement altogether and use the article retrieved as his reward.

To start, place the dog in the down position and walk away from him about fifty feet or so, placing his favorite article on the ground. If you find it easier, for this sequence only, you may wish to start out using pieces of meat as previously mentioned. Once you have placed the article or food on the ground, return to your dog and give him the command *go*, pointing in the direction of the article. Prompt him and encourage him to leave you and go after the item. Once he has reached the spot and located the item, make him stay there. Walk up to him and praise him. Never recall your dog in this exercise, as you want him to stay where the article is without removing it from the location before you check for further evidence. Once the exercise is complete, take the article and play with your partner to reward him for a job well done. Continue this training until you can place different items on the ground and he indicates each one for you without hesitation. He must be willing to leave your side and go instantly in the indicated direction on command.

Once he is adept at the *send*, you can introduce the right and left sweep into the command. Take the article out and to the right of your original location. Send the dog straight out and give him the command to *go right* when he reaches a spot adjacent to the article. You will find that if he cannot first locate the item he will look to you for assistance. Instruct him to go right and sweep your arm to the right. Encourage him and keep him excited. Praise him when he succeeds at locating the article. Make him sit at the location until you approach him and give him his reward. Give him lots of praise.

Do the same procedure for the left hand sweep. You may find it easier to send the dog straight out, make him sit and stay, and then redirect him to the left or right once he is paying attention to you again. Remember to always sweep your left hand to the left and your right hand to the right whenever you give the command *go left* or *go right*.

A good idea is to use a solid fenceline to teach this. Place the article on the ground next to the fence; walk about fifty feet back and ten feet to the right of the article. When you send your dog he will be able to go no farther than the fenceline and will not overshoot the area. Remember, do not always leave the article or wiener on the track. Drop it ten feet or so off to one side of the track so he cannot just follow your trail. You want him to search an area, not simply follow a track.

Once he is adept at the send, place articles in an area where he cannot see you doing so. Allow a small period of time to elapse and then bring out the dog to perform the exercise. Gradually increase the time span between the time you plant the articles and the time the dog searches until he is proficient at searching for articles dropped in an area where there is no possibility of human scent trails to follow.

This is a hard exercise to master, but once learned is very useful and looks sharp when done properly by a well-trained team.

Off-lead

Now that you have completed all aspects of obedience training, work extensively for a week or so using every aspect of his training. Work him until he shows confidence and vigor at every move. Once he shows that confidence, it is time to remove the physical bond between you, and begin working off-lead. An ideal way to start is by utilizing a strong length of fishing line tied from the working ring of the choke collar with the other end of the line attached to the hand loop on the lead. Attach the lead to the collar as usual and after setting up your fishing line, start your training sequence.

At some point during the sequence make a great show of removing the leash so the dog feels he is on his own. He will not realize that he is still attached to the base of the lead via the fishing line and will get the impression he is free from you. Should he fail to perform properly or attempt to take advantage of his new-found freedom, you can effectively snap him back to reality with your fishing line lead.

Continue your training until you are confident that your partner will always obey your commands whether he thinks he is on or off the leash. At this point start your off-lead training and revert to using the fishing line only if you encounter problems.

Work your dog through all of his paces off-lead. Reach down and position him when required and still be solid on corrections if need be. Now is also the time we must implement the *stay* command and work it into his memory. Place him at a sit or down-stay and walk two or three hundred feet away. Give the command to come and allow him to come about fifty feet towards you. Suddenly thrust out your arm, palm forward, and in a loud voice command *stay*. If he stops immediately, praise him. If he continues on, use a loud *no* and make sure your tone of voice attracts his attention. Give the command *stay* again and ensure he stops. Repeat this procedure until he stops instantly. Practice this exercise until you can make him cease any activity and stop dead in his tracks. You should feel confident enough that if your partner were on the opposite side of a busy street and was about to run into the path of oncoming traffic, a single command would keep him safe on the other side until the danger had passed.

Should you have problems teaching him this, a pivot point can be utilized as in the *go* command. Loop the line around a playground goalpost or a flagpole like a pulley, so that as the dog is coming towards you, you can exert pressure on the line (simply by closing your hand on it) and stop him instantly while giving the command *stay*. Once he learns the command, revert to the off-lead training.

Utilize off-lead training by going through your regular training program entirely off-lead. At first you can implement the traffic lead as a "drag factor" to give the dog the impression of direct control, but once you feel confident in his attentiveness, remove the lead and do the whole routine without any attachments. Start out in a location that offers no distractions and eventually work your way into multiple and varied distractions and areas which are new to the dog.

With any problems you encounter off-lead, immediately revert to on-lead training and do it over from the beginning of the sequence you had difficulty with. If necessary, break the training down into steps that are easier for your partner to understand.

Hand Signals

Hand signals should be implemented first during on-line training, and then reinforced during off-lead training. Teaching hand signals during on-line training allows you to instantly enforce the visual commands and gives the dog no freedom to disobey. Once properly associated to the appropriate movements, the hand signals are implemented into the off-lead training program. Again, it is simply an association of your body movement to the command desired. This association will soon cue the dog so that he will become a precision working dog without you giving a single verbal command.

The use of the hand signals becomes very practical in police service work as quite often you and your dog must work in circumstances involving loud machinery. At times the distances separating you from your partner will necessitate visual rather than voice commands, and special operations may also require you to work in silence.

These hand signals can easily be taught to your partner if, from the time he is a young puppy, you make it a habit to implement them every time you give a command. He will learn to observe and obey your hand indications as easily and instantly as your voice commands. If you have not raised your dog from a young age, these commands can still be learned equally well by the animal; it will just take a bit more time to obtain the instantaneous reactions you require.

Throughout your advanced training, as in puppy training, utilize hand signals with every basic obedience voice command. Our methods of obedience training up to this point have required the animal to watch us closely at all times. If you stop, he stops; if he isn't paying attention and continues walking, he gets a heavy choke-chain correction. Through this and other similar experiences he has learned to pay close attention for any clues which might disclose our next intentions. This attentiveness, if taken advantage of by implementing hand signals during regular voice command and obedience training, will make visual command training extremely easy and natural for the dog to pick up. Hand signals can be used for *sit, down, come, stay,* and *go.* (Other non-verbal cues by body movement, such as the foot you step off with meaning *stay* or *heel,* and touch commands for threaten and attack sequences of training, are discussed in the appropriate chapters.)

Keep in mind that at distances your dog is better able to detect movement than to distinguish between objects. Therefore you will find that your hand commands need to be exaggerated more as the distance between you and your partner increases. For this reason, hand signals are done in sweeping motions with the hand. For example, to give the command to sit, sweep your hand upwards in front of you, arm fully outstretched and palm facing outwards, until your hand is above the level of your face. At the same time give him the voice command *sit.* When he completes the movement, drop your arm to a natural position again and immediately praise your dog. To place your dog in the down position lift your arm above your face and in the same fluid motion, sweep your arm downward in front of you, extending your arm down below your waist towards your knees. The palm should

be facing down towards the knee and about forty-five degrees from your body. Again, if voice reinforcement is required, give the command *down*. Repeat the exercises until he cues in on the hand signals only. Have him return to the sit position from the down, and vice versa. Once he knows what is required of him, be firm with your corrections. If he doesn't go down on the assigned signal, correct him accordingly.

The next two hand signals can be taught in the same way. Leaving your dog in the sit-stay position, walk away and turn towards him. Sweep your right hand up towards your body across your chest. The palm of your hand should come to rest touching your left shoulder. At the same time give your dog the verbal command *come*. Continue this phase of training until the dog is self-assured with the *come* signal before going on to the *stay* routine. This will help to prevent any confusion.

To implement the *stay* hand signal, we will start out commanding the dog to come using the visual command only. In mid-route, quickly thrust your right arm outwards towards the dog, palm out, and simultaneously voice the command *stay*. Be sure he stops instantly on command and correct him immediately if he fails to comply. If he persists in wandering forward or inching ahead after you have given him the command, it may be in order to utilize the thirty-foot lead and a pivot point. Repeat the procedure with the line attached. When the command is given for him to stay, stop him with a solid choke-chain correction by seizing the line and pulling sharply. The correction will be transmitted via the pivot point to the dog and will effectively cease his forward motion and at the same time administer a solid correction for his failure to obey. Continue the sequence until you can eliminate all voice commands and get instant response from your partner.

Use the various signal commands in different sequences to prevent anticipation by the dog. Do some exercises utilizing only visual commands and be firm with your corrections.

As your training continues, keep him sharp on the hand signals and all aspects of his obedience. He will be a pleasure to work with and an impressive animal to watch. *The goal is to have maximum control with minimum effort.*

Obstacles

The ability of your dog to overcome obstacles in the field will become vitally important during the pursuit of suspects. Now that we have laid the foundation for communication with the dog, we can advance to the next practical stage of training. We will start by teaching him how to jump, and from there we will advance to other aspects of the agility course. The purpose of the course is to build the animal's confidence in himself and in his physical capabilities, as well as his trust in his handler.

During all phases of agility training, particularly when your partner is working at some height, make certain he never has the opportunity to injure himself. If he slips from a ladder or off a high plank, always be there to catch him. Never put yourself in a position where you will be unable to protect your dog. One bad fall will not only risk physical injury to the dog; his new fear of falling again, and his loss of trust in you as a spotter will also set back your training schedule.

Hup

Start out with a low, solid jump that the dog cannot go under. A jump two feet in height is plenty to begin with, and you will not have to worry about giving him a great distance to gain momentum as he will practically be able to walk over it. Put your dog into a heel routine and increase your pace to a slow jog as you approach the jump. As you reach the jumpoff point give him the command *hup*. Jump over the obstacle with him. If he balks, encourage him over the jump verbally and by guiding him with the lead. If you persevere, it won't be long before you have a jumper. I have found that once dogs have learned what is desired, one of their favorite games is to retrieve articles thrown over a jump. Just remember to keep it a game for your partner. Keep him excited about it and he will learn to love it.

Once you have mastered the two-foot jump, add on another foot or so of height. Although you may not find it feasible to jump with the dog, you can follow the same routine until you reach the jump and give the *hup* command. Once the dog has completed the jump, give him lots of praise. Implement a ball for him to chase over the jumps, giving commands at the appropriate times. Change the procedure when he is confident, so that he must sit a few feet in front of the jump and vault the obstacle with only a short approach distance. This will teach him that he is in fact quite capable of handling obstacles without a great distance to gain momentum.

As he becomes confident at each level, increase the height of the jump approximately six inches at a time. Build his confidence until he is secure in overcoming each new level. Remember, though, that jumping takes a lot of effort on the dog's part and he may tire quickly. Do not overwork him as this may cause injuries. Give him a good break when he starts to tire out. If he has problems and starts to hesitate at a particular height, decrease the size of the jump and start again at the previous level. Do not expect too much from your dog as he will only be able to attain certain heights. Find out what he is capable of and don't push him any further. At greater heights I would strongly recommend that landing ramps be built for the dog to drop onto. These ramps are built to vary in height as required and are designed to shorten the distance the dog drops once over the jump. This prevents strain and injury.

Jumps six feet in height are more than adequate, although the German Shepherd has been known to scale walls in excess of eleven feet. For the greater height requirements your dog will be using you, the handler, as a jumpoff point. He will be taught to jump through a window or over a fence using your back as a stepping stone.

Agility Course

The agility course should be constructed in a manner which challenges all the dog's physical and mental attributes. Start with a series of three or four jumps of varying heights and styles. At least one jump should be made to look like a hedge approximately three feet in height, and another should be constructed in such a manner that you can increase or decrease the height as required.

The next obstacle I prefer is a plank approximately eight feet long and ten inches wide, suspended horizontally between two platforms about six feet off the ground. A set of stairs with wooden steps, similar to those on a child's slide, should be built onto one side of the obstacle, leading to the platform at a medium-to-steep incline. A ramp the same width as the platform should be mounted on the opposite end of the obstacle leading to the ground, at a similar incline. This ramp should be fitted with a non-slip material, to prevent splinters and to give the dog a confident grip.

A window jump should be built so that you are capable of varying the window sill from three to five feet off the ground. It should have the appearance of a window three feet by three feet square and should sit on solid foundations. There should be two boxes constructed for the dog to use as jumpoff points. These can be positioned side by side in front of the window like steps. The purpose of these will become apparent later in the module.

A series of short and long tunnels, utilizing culvert piping, can be installed with minimum effort. A short tunnel constructed of wood, with a turn built into it and a trap door in the roof on either side of the corner, is also a good way to start training your dog for going through culverts. The tunnel should be made three feet square with the first and second legs of the tunnel each only six feet in length. The trap doors can be opened and are intended to assist you in coaxing the dog through.

Six forty-five-gallon drums coated with enamel paint, rolled onto their sides and placed in a pyramid formation offer an excellent obstacle; the slightly slippery surface will teach the dog how to overcome difficult footing situations. A revolving teeter-totter on which the dog can stand and be turned, lifted or lowered is also a good confidence builder.

Almost any type of obstacle can be used or built for your specific needs. Make sure that the obstacle is both well-designed and well-constructed so that you can stay close to your partner at all times while he is going through

it, and there is no danger of him snagging himself or suffering injury due to construction flaws.

As you start your dog on the course, utilize the jumps to build his confidence. When you are satisfied with his work on the jumps introduce him to the window jump at the three-foot level. Once he has mastered jumping through the window, move it up to the five-foot level and place the two steps in front of it. Have him do the jump like this repeatedly during every obedience session. Make sure there is an adequate platform for him to land on opposite the jump. Work your dog until he will jump over any obstacle with your one command.

Now that he is sure of himself, we remove the step closest to the sill and put an assistant trainer in that position, bent over so that his back acts as the step. Move your dog into position, run with him towards the obstacle and give him the command at the appropriate time. He will likely have to be convinced that under these circumstances it is all right to step on a human being. Encourage him and utilize your lead to guide him through if necessary. Make a game of it. It is important that the other trainer brace himself properly so he doesn't move when the dog puts his full weight on him, as your dog will not like using something that gives him uneasy footing. Continue training until he is confident, then remove the first step as well. If you are having extreme difficulty with this exercise, utilize both steps in addition to the man's back to break it down into easier steps for your partner. Keep building your dog's confidence and give him lots of support. Remember, all along you have taught him to respect people by not jumping on them and now you are trying to get him to break that taboo. It will take patience and you must remember to think as the dog does. Everything you do affects him on his level.

The next step is to replace that other trainer with yourself. Position the dog as usual, set yourself in position and give him the command to jump. At the same time pat your back to encourage him on. Again, use the steps as a natural progression and, if necessary, the other trainer may assist you by guiding the dog over the obstacle. This training will become useful in situations where it is inconvenient to lift your partner over an extra-high fence or into a first-storey window after a break-and-enter suspect. (Always keep in mind the danger of broken glass when working on the streets, and if there is any possibility of your dog getting injured, find another way in.)

Another way of teaching your partner to jump off your back is to utilize a wall jump with removable slats. Start by having the dog jump over the wall at a relatively small height and gradually increase it. Place the assistant trainer in a bent-over position beside the wall while it is just slightly higher than the bent-over man, and encourage your dog to jump the man and the wall. Move the slats up the wall gradually, and continue to use the assistant trainer as a jumpoff point until your dog has no difficulty in scaling it to a height of eight feet or so. Take the assistant's place and give the dog the command to jump, simultaneously patting your back to coax him up. If necessary, lower the wall again until your partner is confident and knows it is all right to jump on your back. Encourage him and let him know you are working together as a team. Praise him enthusiastically when he succeeds. Gradually raise the wall and continue practicing until your partner will scale any obstacle using you as a jumpoff point.

Once this training is perfected, you as a team will be able to overcome any obstacles your suspect can jump over. You will also be able to gain ground on him by doing it much faster.

The steps, platforms, plank, and ramp can be used from either end with the dog learning how to climb up and down steep narrow steps, or run up and down a ramp on a steep incline. Use your six-foot lead to guide him up the steps. This will take a lot of encouragement. leave the lead on to give him the feeling of control. Make sure you spot your dog and if he starts to fall, catch him. Spot his feet on the ladder if necessary and praise him instantly for every success, no matter how small. Once he has reached the platform allow him to rest. Go up alongside him and reward him for a job well done. Now encourage him across the plank. Make sure you are beside him all the way.

Use this exercise to build his confidence and trust in you. He will learn that he can trust you to break or prevent his fall if he gets into trouble and this will strengthen your bond. This exercise will build his confidence at working high off the ground in a normally uncomfortable situation as well as his ability to climb on unstable objects.

The tunnels are designed to get him accustomed to crawling through confined and unusual spaces. The wooden tunnel with trap doors described earlier can be used to build the dog's confidence before you progress to the lengthier culverts. To encourage him into these tunnels, call to him from the opposite end or throw his ball in for him to search out.

During all phases of agility training, stress safety for your partner. After building him up to this level you can't afford to set his training back with fear or injury incurred by a fall or improper preparation.

Playtime

Playtime is very important to both the mental and physical health of your dog, and helps to build the bond between you. After every training session or workout in the field I also use a command to let him know that work is over, and playtime has begun and anything goes. The command I use is *split*. When he hears that he almost invariably goes into a play bow, grabs his ball or starts running in circles looking for something to play fetch with. Use this special time whenever you can. It is the best reward you can give your partner.

Postscript

You will find as you progress that your dog will learn to do things automatically without your commands. For instance, my dog automatically lies down in the back of the car every time the car goes into reverse. This is a result of my training him to down so that I could see out the rear window, and was easily accomplished by giving him the command to down every time I backed my car up in our daily routine. Keep this in mind as you train, and make his training a part of your daily life. He will soon start to respond as if he knows precisely what you want and when you want it, without any indication from you. When he does so, praise him. You are well on your way to having a partner who understands and communicates with you.

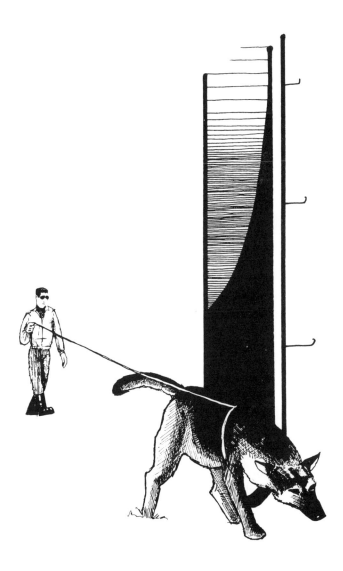

Tracking
and Area Searches

Scent and Scent Characteristics

Before discussing how to train the K9 to track for us, we should study scent and how it is utilized by the dog.

There are three human sweat glands which are important for K9 applications: the eccrine, the emotional eccrine and the apocrine.

Eccrine glands are the body's cooling system and are found throughout the body.

Apocrine glands are located in the palms, nipples, armpits and groin. Scent is stored at these locations until produced by fear or high emotion.

Every person's scent is like a fingerprint, each with its own unique traits. The individual's race, sex, weight and body composition all play a part in forming his scent characteristics. A dog perceives this scent when individual molecules are taken into the turbinate bones and olfactory scrollwork of the dog's nose, where they come into contact with the olfactory cells. The combination of this scent then passes through the olfactory bulb, which distinguishes between different scents, and goes on to the smell memory part of the animal's brain.

The animal has the distinct capability, utilizing this system, of separating different scents. For example, if we take three separate chemicals and mix them together, we as humans would only smell one distinct and possibly foul odor. The canine, on the other hand, has the ability to discern three separate chemical odors.

This attribute, along with the dog's 7000 square millimetres of olfactory cells (as compared to 500 square millimetres in a human) demonstrates the value and abilities these animals have as tracking and search dogs.

When a person runs from the scene of a crime, his emotional and physical state causes the sweat glands to produce large amounts of scent, apocrine and emotional eccrine. As the suspect moves along, this scent hangs in the air wherever he goes, leaving a scent "tunnel." This airborne scent is usually very strong to the dog and gets stronger and easier to follow the closer the animal gets to the suspect, but is quick to dissipate in the slightest breeze or air circulation.

Contact scent is a scent created by the suspect's direct contact with the ground or surrounding buildings, bush, and so on. This contact scent is useful when a lengthy period of time has elapsed since the offender left the scene. The dog uses contact scent together with the concept of transfer: when the suspect walks across different ground surfaces, e.g., grass to pavement to cement, minute particles of grass molecules are carried over to the pavement, and oils and pebbles from the pavement as well as more grass molecules are deposited onto the cement.

Contact scent also makes use of fresh crushed vegetation, broken branches, fresh broken dirt and other similar indications. The dog follows not the scent of the person, as much as the trail of fresh and transferred scents caused when the suspect disturbs the ground as he flees. This contact scent may last for hours.

To add to normal airborne and contact scent, every human being continually sheds dry or dead skin in minute particles called "rafts." These rafts fall to the ground as well as onto surrounding objects and will hold the individual's characteristic scent, easily detected by the K9. The more contact the person has with his surroundings, the more scent left for the animal to work with. Therefore, the denser the grass, bush or other area the better the chances for success.

Regarding moisture and scent characteristics, remember that heavy rains can wash scent away, whereas light rains, dew, or moisture can enhance scent. Dry, intense heat will cause scent to rapidly evaporate, thereby reducing the odors available, but if the area is contained, and the handler waits until evening when the earth is warmer than the surrounding air and the ground becomes slightly moist, the scent will frequently reappear and become usable.

Tasted Scent

Your dog should be monitored closely for dehydration as moist nose lining must be maintained in order for the dog to scent. Also, there is a soft tissue gland in the roof of the mouth of your dog, the vomeronasal gland. This gland is located between the upper canine teeth and extends back on the roof of the mouth. It is slightly softer than the rest of the mouth and should be checked periodically for injury or swelling. Although it serves largely for taste, it is connected directly to the olfactory lobes of the brain. This enhances the dog's ability to track scents from tasted articles.

The lock and key principle is a theory of scent. Simply stated, dogs have receptors into which the actual physical particles of odors fit precisely. There may be thousands of various "keys" which form a particular odor or scent, and dogs can discern any particular pattern and recall it from memory if required.

My own belief is that each scent does consist of a particular pattern of molecules which distinguishes it from all others. Every time a combination of molecules becomes attached to the olfactory cells of the dog's turbinate bones, together with other molecular combinations, the dog distinguishes each combination and stores it in his memory. If the dog is seeking a particular scent, he is able to sort out the various odors coming into contact with the turbinate bones, and to follow the path in which the scent he is seeking remains the strongest.

The heat flow in the human body is from the feet up, so that as the person moves along, body heat flows upward, carrying scent with it. Most scent, other than contact scent, will therefore be approximately one foot above the suspect's head, as scent is the strongest off the forehead. It will then have a tendency to fall from the individual in an almost conical formation, leaving a "tunnel" of scent behind the suspect as he proceeds.

Points to Remember When Tracking

1. A tracking dog's use of contact scent is aided by the occurrence of transfer (with crushed grass and so on) and is therefore severely limited in urban areas. Usually on asphalt, time is of the essence, as only air or tunnel scents can be detected because of rapid contamination.

2. The air-scenting or trailing dog utilizes winds and air circulation to scent. Take full advantage of the downwind side whenever possible, particularly during area searches.

3. Backtrack to search for dropped or discarded evidence. Your K9 will indicate articles which are foreign to the area, e.g., a gun discarded in grass.

4. Remember that scent can be trapped by fresh snow, ice or frost and when this scent is released by thawing it can still be utilized and tracked by the dog after many hours.

5. Be cautious of dead spots in which the dog may appear to have lost the scent; the scent may actually have been briefly interrupted by air currents. The same situation applies where scents are concentrated in one location because of currents. The dog may not want to leave because he feels the suspect is close. Work as a team. Realize that though the dog is "hot," it may be advisable to cast around again.

6. During building searches, be aware of the chimney effect, where the scent rises from the suspect, floats across the ceiling and drops down. The suspect may be directly opposite to where the dog is indicating.

7. Be cautious of winds between buildings which blow perpendicular to the track. They will disperse and distort the scent and may set your dog off-track.

8. You may find that your dog will sometimes track twenty to thirty feet off the actual track. This is usually because he is utilizing tunnel scent off the individual rather than ground contact scent, and the suspect's scent has drifted due to a slight breeze or air current.

9. Scent will often drift until caught in tall grass, bush, or along the low side of a ditch or embankment. Once caught, the scent may be preserved in the area, and the dog will track along until he approaches the suspect. As the dog closes in on the intended quarry, the scent cone will become more distinct and uniform, allowing the dog to close in rapidly.

10. When a suspect or quarry crosses a stream or body of water, the scent dissipates into the air currents above the water. This air current is caused by the flow of the stream or by the difference between land temperature and water temperature. Although the dog cannot track across the water, another phenomenon also occurs which can be used to your advantage. Where scent has dissipated over water, it will roll into the banks on each side of the body of water and remain very concentrated in most circumstances. By casting along the bank of the stream, the dog can locate the entry and exit points to and from the stream and may then continue on the track.

Note: Some people, although very few, do not sweat; others do not produce scent and therefore cannot easily be tracked. Because of this, lost young children may be more difficult to track, and contact scent must be utilized over air scenting. The very young and very old will not generate apocrine scents *as their apocrine systems do not produce.* This should be kept in mind by the handler. If searching areas for a lost person of this age or category, it may be applicable to work smaller grids.

Track Training Concept

Most police forces I have observed or trained with have similar ideas as to how to teach their dogs to track. This is to gradually work the animal up in his distance by making the tracks longer as the dog progresses. The method starts out with the handler taking the dog's favorite article, walking out about 100 feet or so, placing it on the ground and then returning to the dog on the same track. The K9 trainee is then sent to find the article, usually successfully. This progression continues, eventually substituting a quarry with no return track, and the find of the quarry at the end of the track being the reward for the dog.

On the street I find most police service dogs track very well, but some have a greater tendency to use tunnel scent than contact scent. Once onto the tunnel scent the dog gets "hot" as he knows he is closing on the suspect, but suddenly, particularly if there is a slight breeze or traffic movement nearby causing air circulation, the dog loses the trail and overshoots where the suspect turned off. It is then necessary to cast around again to pick up the trail, and the dog will often be unsuccessful.

What is happening here? The dog knows how to track. He was on the trail and getting close but suddenly lost the trail and wasn't able to pick it up.

Most PSDs are on the scene of the crime within minutes. They are usually in time to utilize tunnel or airborne scent, or they are able to track the first part of the trail and switch to air-scenting as they close in on the suspect. Even in their basic training, the dogs air-scent, first to locate their handler during hide and seek exercises, then to follow the scent to where an article or toy is dropped, and finally to find their quarry. They resort to putting their noses down only to start the track and if they are unable to air-scent.

Herein lies the problem. Most service dogs are not keen on methodical tracking of contact scent. Dogs and their handlers track suspects until they hit concrete or pavement and then run into trouble because they have become used to air-scenting. The usual procedure is to find the direction in which the suspect has most likely gone and start the dog casting around again. This is a fault of neither dog nor handler. It simply results from the large number of airborne trails the dog first learned to track by, combined with the high percentage of criminal apprehensions from crime scenes where the team arrives quickly enough to utilize the airborne scent. The dog's use of contact scent is not stressed in training and is therefore limited, since he air-scents and most departments utilize this natural attribute in training the dogs to track.

The concept I will instruct in this module is to teach the dog to track methodically using contact scent. Only when he is successfully able to track contact scent across any surface will we introduce the quarry near the end of the track so that the dog can then lift his head, utilize the airborne scent and close in on the suspect.

When the dog is capable of accurate contact scent tracking, you will find that if there is some uncertainty as to the airborne trail, the dog will automatically revert to tracking without casting and without the handler having to slow the dog down. This approach is intended to produce a versatile and precise tracker, retaining all the desirable traits of the present police service dogs while improving the animal's ability to track through contaminated and difficult locations. This will be particularly useful in urban areas.

The other advantage to training the dog to track precisely before introducing the quarry is that the animal is often so anxious to get a bite on the suspect that it tends to lose concentration during the track as it thinks of the end result. Thus if the team is air-scenting and the suspect incorporates a sharp turn as the dog closes in, and there is wind in the area, the dog may lose the trail entirely, as he is "hot" and does not put his nose to the ground to make use of the available contact scent. In his excitement he loses the track entirely when in reality he is very close to success. Conventional track training, then, can give rise to several kinds of problems in street situations.

For this reason we will not start our agitation training until after the dog is capable of accurate tracking, and has learned to find a quarry without a resulting attack.

Teamwork/Mantracking

There will be times when, due to atmospheric conditions, area contamination or other circumstances, your K9 will run into difficulty tracking a suspect. We must learn not to depend entirely on the dog to do the job for us, but to do a bit of mantracking ourselves. A suspect who has committed a crime and is under stress can be very predictable.

There are two basic types of tracks which will concern us — the passive track and the active track. For criminal apprehension the active track is the one we will deal with in most circumstances. In this case, the quarry is under a lot of pressure to avoid apprehension. Fleeing suspects have a tendency to follow certain patterns, some of which are as follows:

— suspects will make efforts to employ continual left turns.

— if the suspect attempts to hide within a large building he usually stays near the outside walls.

— if there are two suspects and they are forced to "go to ground," one suspect will usually be within 200 to 300 feet of the other.

— one suspect will usually stay in the area if the other is caught, to see what the outcome is.

— most evidence discarded by suspects is found on the right side of the track.

This information has been accrued by the writer through various seminars and personal experience. In experiments where quarries re-enacted the crime scene and were told to make all efforts to escape detection it was found that given the same set of circumstances each time, the quarries would take a route very similar to that of the original suspect. Take the time to use this predictability to your advantage.

Passive tracks are those in which the subject being sought is under no pressure to avoid detection. The scent left may consequently be less dense. Such are the circumstances when dealing with lost or missing persons. Again, certain visible signs or likely circumstances may assist you in trailing such an individual. As in the active tracks, most subjects when faced with an obstacle will go to the right. If you are searching for children, they tend to doddle, drag their feet, and stop quite frequently to investigate their surroundings. Children and women are said to prefer uphill routes whereas men will travel downhill. In direct contrast to active tracks which turn generally to the left and then to the right in sharp attempts to avoid detection, passive tracks usually sweep gradually to the right over large distances.

Mantracking is not something which can be learned overnight and a great many hours of practice are required for anyone to become very adept at it. It requires many hours and great patience to cover only small distances but the rewards make the effort quite worthwhile. Take the time to have someone lay a few tracks for you each week. Make them short distances and track them without the use of the dog. Watch for the lay of the grass and for wet footprints from the dew or in the frost.

Recently, without the use of my dog, I had to track a trail left in the frost along two blocks of sidewalk, across two roadways and over some lawns. The total length of the track was four blocks, and although not visible from a normal point of view, it became lightly but plainly visible when I bent close to the ground and shone my streamlight above the area of the trail. It took me three hours to cover the four blocks, and I finally lost the track as the sun came up and the early morning mist wiped out the trail. Further neighborhood enquiries resulted in the arrest of the burglary suspect and the recovery of the property. I had mantracked the subject to within a half block of his residence.

The point I want to emphasize is that you as the handler are often capable of seeing evidence the dog does not detect, or you may come to a point where you can make a logical decision as to where the track continues from where the dog leaves off. Becoming proficient at mantracking takes a lot of time, patience and perseverence. I strongly recommend that those who will be using their dogs for tracking a great deal should also obtain whatever literature they can on mantracking and become well-read on the subject. It can make the difference between success and failure for difficult tracks encountered throughout a team's career.

Remember, tracking is teamwork, involving both you and your dog's ability to track, as well as your ability as a dog handler to read the subtle clues your dog is providing. Mantracking evidence in court which connects the end of a track and the detection of a fresh track by your dog is accepted when you can prove to the courts your abilities as a tracker. Communication between you and your partner, proper application of mantracking techniques, and proper presentation of the evidence in court can bring great success.

Equipment

For our purposes we will utilize a thirty-foot longe line and tracking harness. I prefer to use a harness which forms a "V" on the animal's chest rather than the style which goes straight across the front of the chest. The latter type puts a lot of pressure on the dog's chest as he pulls along and

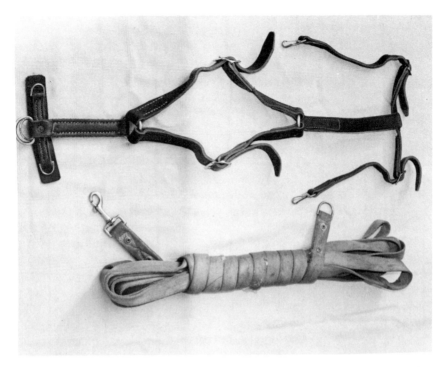

tends to rub on his front shoulder, which will cause him some discomfort on extended tracks. The V-type harness fits into the natural grooves of the dog's chest and neck. The animal suffers no discomfort, and therefore will be able to track more energetically.

As mentioned in Chapter 7, reflective material can be incorporated into the harness to add to the dog's visibility in traffic and in darkness. One style of harness even includes a three-inch nipple of reflective material which folds down when bumped against heavy bush to prevent the dog from getting hung up, but springs back to its original erect position for easy visibility for the handler.

Whether or not you use a harness on the dog when on the street is entirely up to you. During training, the use of the harness and line assists us in teaching the dog methodical tracking styles. You will find also that as training progresses the dog will automatically put his nose down to look for a track whenever you start to put on his harness. As such, the harness can also be used to cue the dog for off-line area searches.

My own preference on the street is on-line work for tracks involving lengthy time delays, and off-line work or "free tracking" for area searches and incidents with short time delays. The on-line tracking method allows me to maintain continuity for track evidence in court, as I never lose sight of the dog. Should you allow the dog to free-track you may lose sight of him, and your track continuity could be lost. This is not to say that free tracks cannot or should not be done, as I have used both methods with excellent results; the dog on free tracks can be easily taught to stay within proper distance of you by voice control. The decision is yours as to which style you use. Both on-line and off-line tracks will be taught within this module to satisfy the proponents of both methods. The advantages and disadvantages of each style will be covered as the module progresses.

Stage One — Basic Nosework

As you raise your puppy you will use basic terms for commands which will assist you in future training. To this end you should be taking his ball, or another favorite toy, and while leaving the dog on a stay, let him watch you walking away and hiding it in some grass or light bush area. This type of terrain allows an easy track for the pup and is a good confidence builder.

Once you have hidden the ball in the grass, walk back to your dog and give him the command *search lost*. Be excited and make a game of it for him. If this is truly his favorite article, it won't be long before he has located it successfully. When he does, praise him for it. Impress this command to search upon him every chance you get. Extend the distance of the track and the time you make him wait. When he is proficient at retrieving the article, switch to a new article which is strange to him, yet easy to fetch and retrieve, such as a purse. This simple game, when associated with the search command, will soon mean something to the pup and make the advanced training much easier.

Another game which provides excellent preparation for your pup prior to formal training is that of hide and seek. Have an assistant hold the dog on a lead. If he is big enough you should apply the tracking harness to the dog so that he begins to cue to it as an indication of the task at hand. Once he is prepared, you as his handler should tease him, play with him and then run off into the bush in plain view so the pup can see exactly where you are going. As you go, call out to him in an effort to excite him into chasing after you. As you enter the bush he will lose sight of you and will have to utilize his olfactory capabilities to find you. Work your way into the bush a hundred yards or so, turn sharply to the left or to the right and hide about 100 feet or so off the main track. After a predetermined time your assistant releases the dog and encourages him to search for you by using the command *search*. If necessary, maintain the animal's interest during this initial training by calling out to him from your position. As you continue this form of hide and seek you may extend the distances and incorporate more complicated terrain and a larger number of turns.

Once your pup has mastered the ability to locate you during hide and seek and to seek out and retrieve balls, purses and other articles, it is time to move onto the next stage of training. Be sure to use your commands frequently so the pup learns exactly what they mean. Of great importance during track and search training is that the dog enjoys what he is doing and that it is always a game in which his success reaps reward. Try to avoid using other commands or scolding your partner when he is tracking, and above all learn to trust his abilities rather than your own instincts. Often we may call the dog off because the witnesses say the suspect turned in a different direction or because our own instincts tell us we are on the wrong track, only to learn later that the dog had been on the proper track. This is one of the most common causes of failure in the field.

Stage Two

Once the dog understands what the command to search means, it is time to hide the articles we have been using without him observing where we are going. When hiding an article, make sure to come out on the same track you went in on. This form of double-tracking allows the dog that much more scent to work with until he is confident. Place the dog on harness and command him to search. When he locates the proper track you will note an instant change in his demeanor. This is called his "indication." His nose will go down, his tail will be out from his body and he will use his nose vigorously. Praise him enough to let him know you are pleased, but do

not distract him. Follow him until he finds the article and praise him thoroughly.

Make the first tracks "one-leg" tracks, meaning that there will be no turns implemented. It should be approximately 100 yards in length and as the training advances, you should allow time for some of the scent to dissipate. This will make the track more challenging to the dog. Attach the harness and longe line to the dog and encourage him to track by using the command *search*. Be very cautious how you use the tracking line. It should be handled smoothly and gently to prevent unnecessary strain on the dog. Keep the line taut without restricting him and avoid sudden jerks as it will adversely affect your partner. When the dog starts the track, work your line at full length and never use your line to correct him.

As the dog succeeds at locating the articles at the end of each track, increase the time delay to ten, then fifteen minutes, and so on until he can successfully track vegetation tracks up to an hour old. If he is still confident, continue to increase the delay until you know your partner's limit. Don't forget that atmospheric and ground conditions produce many variables and should be noted in the dog log (see Chapter 16) for future reference. Do the same series of tracks in a wide open park or field on days when there is a breeze blowing. The track should be laid with the wind so that the dog cannot air-scent. The breeze will cause the air scent to dissipate, forcing the dog to put his nose down in order to track and retrieve the article successfully. This is the first step to accurate contact-scent nosework. As with the previous tracks, increase the distances and the time delays.

The next step is to have an assistant place the article at the end of a two-leg track. This is a track where the first leg is about 400 yards in length, with the quarry laying a scent pad and then making a ninety-degree turn to the left or right and proceeding to where he drops the article or hides at the end of the second leg. The "scent pad" is simply a small area where an extra effort is made to leave a lot of scent, by stamping or rubbing the feet. Should the dog overshoot the corner during his tracking of the quarry, it will enable him to locate the corner a little more easily. Continue this training until the dog can successfully complete four or even five legs and retrieve or indicate two or three articles left at different places along the trail. This teaches the dog that the track does not necessarily end when he finds the first article. His greatest reward should always be the last article placed on the track. When he locates each article, have him either retrieve it to you, sit, or speak until you have recovered the article. You must choose whatever form of indication is preferable for your purposes. Obviously an officer training his partner in the basics of bomb detection would want him to indicate by sitting rather than by retrieving!

Praise your dog consistently at the conclusion of each successful exercise and make him feel your excitement. Your satisfaction is his greatest joy. With the proper amounts of praise, encouragement and playtime, your partner will produce very reliable results.

Up to this point our training has been directed at teaching the dog to relate to a specific action, e.g., searching in response to a given command. As you know, the dog has the ability to use his nose instinctively to locate what he is looking for. The above sequences are used as games to get him to use those special abilities for us. We are training him not how to search or track but rather when to search and when to track for a particular item or person.

Stage Three

For the basics of track training we will now use the longe line attached to the tracking harness and start to associate the different types of tracks with different commands. When beginning a track for a suspect or a lost person I utilize the command *search*. During off-line area searches for lost or discarded articles I prefer the command *search lost*. For drug searches I use a third command, *search dope*. In each case the key command which starts the dog to work is *search*. The subsequent command is to give him an idea as to what specific item he is searching for.

With repeated application of the commands to different situations you will find that your partner will easily perform the task at hand without any confusion whatsoever over the various cues. You will find that he will become very adept at locating hidden articles when you use the *search lost* command as he will be accustomed to looking for a very small article. When placed on line and given the command to *search* he will be intent on finding your suspect but will also indicate a dropped or discarded item. Once the article is retrieved by the handler, the dog will continue on until he locates a suspect or loses the trail.

For the basics of all our track training we will now implement the use of the harness and longe line. The thirty-foot longe line is ideal for tracking purposes, affording ample line to work the dog on corners and allowing a comfortable distance between dog and handler. This permits easy handling and control and also prevents possible distraction and confusion caused by the handler being too close to the dog. As we progress to learning area searches and off-line tracking for those who prefer this type of track, the longe line will be removed.

The longe line is the means by which you as the handler communicate to and receive communication from the dog. Improper use of the line can quickly discourage your partner from wanting to work. You must handle the line with gentleness and avoid sudden jerks on the line, no matter how small. What appears to be a light pull on your end of the line is transformed to a heavy jolt on the dog's end of the line. It takes only a couple of these jolts before the dog will tire. An excellent demonstration of this for new handlers is to have them grasp one end of the longe line, drape it over one shoulder and start to walk. An assistant remaining at the starting point takes the line in his hand and allows it to loosely reel out between his palms. At some point the assistant closes his fists and grasps the line firmly. The result usually demonstrates quite effectively to the handler on the receiving end exactly what the effects of his actions are on the dog's end of the lead.

An even more vivid demonstration involves having the handler actually clip the harness onto himself and walk forward while the assistant closes his fists around the line with varying intensity. In this way, the handler gets a thorough understanding of the shock the dog receives every time tension is applied to the line. The principal rule, therefore, is simply to always maintain even tension on the line. Tension is necessary in varying degrees when you are tracking; it is the sudden jerking we wish to avoid.

Apply the harness to your dog and clip on the longe line. The quarry should lay a track in an area that will both be easy to work in with the dog, and afford some degree of cover such as long grass. The quarry should lay a track unobserved by the dog and preferably in a situation where he will not be easily wind-scented. This is in direct contrast to tracking into the wind, which is easier and therefore often used in training the dog to track. Many handlers prefer this method of training, but I find that my dogs use the air scent opportunities too often and have a tendency to become lazy. I recommend therefore that you incorporate tracks which will teach the dog to keep his nose down and to use his abilities to the fullest. As training progresses we will take advantage of wind direction, but for now we want the dog to learn accurate, methodical tracking utilizing contact scent.

The first on-line tracks should be short to allow both the dog and handler to become accustomed to the feel of the line. The point from which the quarry leaves should be well-trodden to leave a scent pad from which the dog may begin. The use of this scent pad will be disposed of as the animal becomes more proficient in tracking procedures.

Have the quarry lay a one-leg track approximately 200 yards in length. With only a short time delay (five minutes or so), take the dog to the vicinity of the scent pad and give him the command *search*. Prompt and encourage him until he indicates the track.

When the dog puts his nose down and starts to follow the trail left by the quarry, praise him and let him know he is doing precisely what you want. As he continues, however, keep the praise to a minimum; in future stages of training you will want to save that praise for when he gives a clear indication of a turn in the trail or he recovers something on the track. You must refrain from using his name or speaking unnecessarily while he is actively tracking, as you want him to concentrate fully on the task at hand. The key is to keep his attention on the track and refrain from doing anything that will divert his attention to you or to anything else. This is another very important example of why the dog must be taught to ignore distractions during the earliest stages of obedience training.

As you start out, allow the longe line to extend freely to its full length. I prefer to keep about three feet or so in reserve which I can release if I get hung up on an obstacle while trying to keep up with my partner. As the end of the longe approaches, gently close your fists around the line slowly and evenly, gradually adding tension to the line until you are holding it firm and maintaining an even pace with your partner. You may find his pace too quick for you to maintain and it is during this initial training that you must work on keeping him at a reasonable pace. You can control this by checking the rate at which he pulls you along. Remember to keep these first tracks short so he does not become discouraged with having to pull you. The idea is to encourage him to check his own pace so that as he advances in training he will maintain that pace.

As your partner tracks along the predetermined trail, take great care to learn how he appears to indicate to you. These indications are the dog's natural body reactions to the activity in which he is involved. These reactions will be consistent in every phase of training. Only when you have learned to read his behavior language in controlled situations will you be able to read and discriminate the subtle clues he may give you in real-life situations where you do not have the advantage of knowing what the true track details are.

When your partner locates the article(s) at the end of the track, make a big show of praising him. If you make it clear that you are pleased with him, he will soon comprehend the connection between a successful track and your praise.

Work numerous tracks with articles placed at the end of the track and slowly start to implement the use of a hidden quarry. Extend the track's length to include an article dropped in the middle of the track, an article near the end of the track and finally the quarry. Make special note of how your dog indicates each article as he tracks, and take this opportunity to begin teaching your dog to indicate in the desired manner. If you are comfortable with the way your dog gives you a positive indication of dropped articles then leave it at that. Some officers train their partners to automatically sit, go down, retrieve or bark when an article is located. My preference for a general duty dog is not to have the dog voice until he has confronted a suspect. My partner will stop and stay when he locates an article until I give him the go-ahead to resume the track. Whatever your personal preference may be, now is the time to implement it into your training program.

Stage Four

Work until your partner is proficient at single-leg tracks involving some distance and numerous articles. When you are confident in your dog, implement a single forty-five degree turn to the left or to the right. As the handler you should know precisely where the turn is by coordinating your tracking plans with the quarry. You may also make use of a small flag mounted on a long piece of wire which is planted into the ground by the quarry at the point of the corner. This should be avoided whenever possible, however, as the dog soon learns to cue on the flag rather than working it out with his nose.

During the first few tracks in which corners are implemented, refrain from placing articles on the track so that the dog remains attentive to the continuous scent.

Set your partner on the track and follow through as you normally do. When your dog reaches the corner allow him to continue past it until he realizes he is no longer on the correct track. Should he take the turn properly, praise him and allow him to go on.

If he overshoots the corner, allow him to continue and note how long it takes him to realize he has lost the trail. Make particular note of the changes in his indications so that you can recall on future tracks how he reacts to a sudden loss of scent. You must learn to recognize this indication change so that you can plant your position accurately at the last known location on the positive track. If you allow the dog to cast in a circle with you as the pivot point, your partner will likely cut across the trail in its new direction and resume the track.

When you stop and plant your feet firmly, your partner has no choice but to stop and circle. Encourage him to search, and maintain an even tension on your longe line. If he works his way back toward you, reel in the line and then allow it to reel out again gradually, always maintaining a light tension to prevent your partner from becoming entangled in the line. Remember, the idea of stopping dead in your tracks when your partner loses the trail is, that you can use your position as a starting point from which the dog can circle and cast for scent. With only thirty feet of longe line it is likely that you have stopped well within the area where the track changed direction.

When stopping to mark the corner, you must remember not to jerk your dog out of his tracks. Apply even tension on the line and utilize the extra five feet of slack to cushion the impact of stopping on your partner. Keep your actions smooth, always maintaining light, even tension on the line, and prevent tangling. Increase the tension gradually if you wish your partner to slow down, until he acknowledges the desired pace and slackens his stride accordingly.

As you stay in position and your partner casts around, allow him to work at the full length of the line. Encourage him to search until he relocates the trail. When his nose goes down and he starts to positively indicate the trail again, praise him accordingly and resume the track. As you become proficient, you will be able to feel a change in the tension of the line when the dog locates or loses the track.

As your partner completes the second leg of the track and locates the quarry, fuss over him and praise him. Should he have difficulty and appear to lose interest near the end of the track, the quarry can hiss or make some other noise to help the dog to find him. Although the track has technically been unsuccessful, the dog's interest has been revitalized and his confidence boosted. He was, in fact, successful to the point where his interest started to wane. Praising him for locating the quarry, even when the quarry has helped him along, impresses upon the dog what the correct end result should be. With the proper amount of encouragement and praise for every successful find, your partner's interest should remain high.

Once you have completed the two-leg track with a turn of forty-five degrees, implement a series of tracks utilizing ninety-degree turns. Follow the same procedures as previously described, ensuring that the quarry leaves a scent pad at the beginning of the track and at the turn. Always keep the second leg of the track short so as to maintain the dog's interest with easy finds until he is confident and accurate in his abilities.

As the dog becomes proficient, extend the track and then implement the use of numerous turns at varying degrees. Restrict yourself to vegetation tracks for the present until you are working extensive distances. Start your tracks with time delays as short as ten minutes, and gradually increase the delays until you can successfully utilize the dog on vegetation tracks up to ninety minutes old. This will assure you that the dog is capable of working entirely on contact scent. As you progress, discontinue the use of the scent pads on the turns, and include discarded articles on the track. Should you find at any point that your partner consistently has difficulty with a certain aspect of the tracking, such as left turns or article indications, work these into your program more frequently.

Remember that at this point you are attempting to impress contact-scent tracking onto the dog, and therefore you want to avoid situations where you are tracking into a wind, which would carry the airborne scent back to the dog. The use of this airborne scent will become an integral part of our tracking course as we progress, but not until the dog is highly proficient at the skills of contact scent tracking.

Stage Five — Advanced On-line Tracks

Up to this point we have worked extensively on vegetation tracks and, more specifically, the use of contact scent. The reason for using vegetation-type tracks is the ease with which the dog is able to follow the trail left by the suspect; the crushed and transferred vegetation always produces large amounts of scent. Should the track be laid entirely on a surface of cement, however, you would find that little or no contact scent is left behind. When the trail changes from one surface to another, we get the best of both: the freshly-crushed vegetation or freshly-scraped surface of the cement, as well as the transferred material (crushed grass on cement, and minute particles of lime from the cement surface deposited on the grass.) This is precisely what we will now work on.

All articles which are moved or touched by another item transfer some material to the article which is contacted, no matter how small that particle may be. For example, a fingerprint on a piece of glass is the result of moisture, salt and other body minerals which are deposited on the glass. The finger also receives a transfer of dust, oil or other grime from the glass surface. In both cases something has been left and something has been taken away. Your partner, if conditioned for the purpose of the experiment, has the ability to enter a glass-filled room, detect and indicate where a solitary fingerprint had been placed on a piece of glass within that room.

Your next step is to condition your dog to track a suspect who covers a wide variety of surfaces and thereby transfers various scents from one surface to another, creating a more difficult, yet still continuous track.

The area used for training should include a paved street with grass or similar vegetation on both sides. The quarry should lay a track as he normally would, and run the track perpendicular to the roadway, crossing the street at exactly a right angle so that the dog has only to track straight across the street to pick up the scent again. Use only a short time delay of ten minutes or so and, if possible, work in conditions where the suspect's airborne scent has had a chance to dissipate before the dog begins the track.

Place the dog on the track and allow him to work as he normally would. Note how he handles the track once he comes upon the pavement, and allow him to work it out. If he starts to stray off, plant your position and have him circle you until he relocates the track. If it is necessary to take him to the opposite side of the road where the track resumes, this is fine.

Praise him when he resumes the track and encourage him until he completes it. As you continue you may frequently find it necessary for you to indicate the tracks on the opposite side. This is quite proper, as it is precisely how you will be required to relocate trails your partner loses anyway, and your dog will learn that the track does in fact continue across the hard surface.

Should your dog continue over the pavement on the trail as if there were no change in surface, praise him once he hits the vegetation on the other side of the road and carry on to complete the track.

As your partner shows proficiency in crossing a hard surface, have your quarry weave around and back over the paved surface two or three times before ending the track. Start the track with longer time delays and have the quarry start dropping articles along the way for your partner to indicate as well. When you are satisfied that he is proficient at this stage, you may advance a step.

The next stage is to have the quarry do the same form of track, except that the track should approach the paved portion at an angle and maintain that angle until he comes onto the vegetation on the opposite side again. As before, these tracks should begin as one-leg tracks and continue to advance in distance as well as in time delays as the dog progresses successfully through each sequence.

At this point the quarry should combine the previous two steps and lay tracks which cross the road at different angles and in different directions. Implement an area where there is a sidewalk between the vegetation and the road, and work the dog on short tracks down the surface of the sidewalk as well.

Streams always prove to be interesting obstacles and should be integrated into your training. As noted previously, although you cannot track across the surface of the water, the dog can locate the ample pockets of scent which curl up around the banks of the stream. Use the very same sequence in training your dog to retain the track continuity across the stream as you did teaching him to do hard-surface tracks. There is a slight difference, however, in the type of track which crosses a stream. We use contact scent up to the edge of the water, reverting to hanging airborne scent to continue the task and then returning to contact scent on the other side.

Stage Six — Cross Tracks

You will on many occasions be forced to use the dog where a moderate amount of pedestrian traffic has crossed over the trail left by your suspect. In most cases your partner will be used to seek out and follow the freshest track leaving the scene of the crime, as this is usually the trail of your suspect. In situations where there is some time delay involved and people cross the area in the normal course of their activities, the most important information you can have is the exact location where the suspect was last seen by a witness or patrol member. Once it has been established, you must make this your starting point.

When the dog has been placed onto a specific track, the ideal situation is for him to stay on that track no matter what other trails go across the original track. Your partner is capable of knowing whether he is on the track of the original suspect, or if he has suddenly turned onto a new track. He does this by discerning the amount of scent which dissipates from each particular trail. Each track has its own unique characteristics. The size and weight of the individual, the type of footwear he is wearing, and the length of his stride all play an important part in distinguishing one track from another. The most important factor, however, is the age of each track. Your dog knows how old the track is and knows when he is gaining and about to close in on the suspect. This is readily visible as you near the end of any track. Your dog will step up his pace, possibly bringing his nose up and breaking into a run as he closes on the suspect by air-scenting on the suspect's tunnel scent.

In the same way, your dog is able to maintain his concentration on the original track, even if it is an hour old, and two or three people have walked across the original track at thirty, forty and fifty minute intervals. Your dog must be trained to maintain the original track and to discard the temptation of tracking a more freshly-laid trail. It is this aspect of contact scent tracking we will now work on.

As in the previous training, we will revert to the single-leg track, but will keep its length extended to at least 400 yards. With a one-leg track, you can discuss with the quarry the precise starting and ending points of his trail so that any deviation from that line will be easily discernible. Have the quarry leave a scent pad the first few times and proceed to lay the track, leaving an article about 200 yards along and another at the end of the track.

When the track is thirty minutes old, have another person walk across the track approximately 100 yards from the starting point, perpendicular to the trail left by the quarry. Allow the track to age another ten minutes or so and then begin the track with your partner.

As the dog approaches the point where the second person cut across the original trail, he may slow, or may suddenly make the turn and proceed along the new track. Maintain your position on the original trail but allow him to deviate a bit to see if he will figure out that he is on the wrong track. Many dogs will turn around and backtrack to the original trail and successfully complete the proper track. We will assume that your partner has deviated from the original track.

You have maintained your position on the original trail and are now 100 yards into the track and about 100 yards from the first dropped article. If your partner is straining to carry on his new trail give him a firm *no* without being harsh and direct him back towards the original track by manipulating the longe line accordingly. Work him back onto the proper trail and command him to search. As he picks up on the track again praise him. Allow him to work his way to the first article and indicate it to you, and then praise him again. Permit him to complete the original track by locating the second article at track's end. This will serve to teach the dog that the proper track is always the one on which he is originally placed and that the fresh trails which cross his path are to be ignored. Only when he stays on track and locates the articles does he receive praise for his work. When he deviates he is not chastised but gently corrected, and is directed back to his proper track and to a successful conclusion.

Repeat the above sequence until your partner is consistent in remaining on the proper track. Advance the trail with a series of cross-tracks at three locations with varying time delays. Continue the same procedures until he is accurately tracking without any deviation. If he turns onto a fresh track and then returns to the original track, this is quite proper. He is simply running across a conflicting trail and must take the time to sort out the problem. Praise him immediately every time he returns to the correct track.

Once your partner is adept at short tracks crossed with conflicting trails, extend your training to include multiple-leg tracks. Again, implement cross-tracks over the original trail at various points, and work your dog through numerous types of surfaces. Continue to use small articles such as wallets for the dog to locate along the route. This training should continue until the dog is capable of tracking consistently over extended distances which are contaminated with cross-tracks. These tracks should involve all surface types the dog will be required to work on once he hits the streets.

Now that your partner is a consistent tracker, the time has come to implement the quarry at the end of every track. Until now, we have had the dog work on contact scent rather than airborne scent in order to reinforce his ability to track over difficult terrain in adverse conditions. Now we will utilize the airborne scent left by the quarry. The quarry will now stay at the end of each track and the dog will be permitted to find him, and subsequently be praised for doing so.

Permitting the dog to air-scent on a track is easily done. You really have nothing to teach the dog. He will easily cue into the airborne scent when he closes on the suspect. As he nears the hiding place of the quarry, the contact scent naturally becomes stronger as the track becomes fresher. At some point the scent will become so strong that the dog will begin to lift his head, quicken his pace and continue to indicate a positive track with his head up. This change in the dog's style of tracking indicates that he has switched from using contact scent to airborne scent. From this point he will close swiftly on the suspect, and you as a police officer should be forewarned that a suspect is close by.

As you continue to lay tracks, combine fresh tracks where the quarry is still at the end of the track with old tracks where only contact scent can be utilized. When you want the dog to keep his nose down, lay the track with the wind. When you want him to pick up the quarry's air scent, lay it into the wind. The age of the track in each circumstance as well as the number of conflicting cross-tracks and the wind direction are entirely up to you. Work the dog until he is always accurate and will put his head down if he overshoots a corner when he wind-scents. You can encourage this by

knowing where the quarry turns off the trail, and by implementing the on-line method of tracking.

Off-line Tracking

Off-line tracking as compared to on-line tracking is simply a matter of personal preference. Once the dog has become a consistent on-line tracker and is familiar with all the commands associated with tracking, you can start to work off-line.

Off-line work requires the ability to verbally control your dog with precision. He must respond to you as accurately off-lead as he would on-lead in order for you to maintain maximum control. Only when you have this degree of control over your partner should you attempt off-line tracking.

There are various advantages and disadvantages to each style of tracking. Some of these are as follows:

On-line Tracks

— allow the handler physical control over the dog and the ability to feel movement and changes in the dog's demeanor through the line.

— assist the handler in maintaining contact with the dog in heavy bush areas, where the dog may be capable of easily slipping through but where the handler has difficulty in keeping up.

— prevent the handler from interrupting the dog with voice commands and thusly eliminate some minimal verbal distraction.

— allow the handler to maintain true track continuity, as he never loses sight of the dog on the track.

— should the dog overshoot a turn in the track and the handler is suddenly attacked by the suspect, the dog is no further than the length of the line away and can return very quickly to assist the handler. A dog which is tracking a distance of 100 feet off-lead may take longer to return and protect the officer.

— on-lead tracking is more accurate as the dog is more adept at picking up turns in the track and will not overshoot as much as in off-line work.

— a handler who is concentrating on working the dog is at a disadvantage for street survival applications. He is usually working close enough to the dog to be within shooting range of a fleeing suspect when he is finally located by the dog.

— the dog can become entangled in the line and be restricted somewhat in a confrontation with a suspect.

— should a confrontation occur while the dog is still some distance from the suspect, the handler cannot easily remove the line. He can send the dog in only by releasing his end of the line. Again this is a hindrance to the animal, particularly in heavy brush.

Off-line Tracks

— the dog is free to work at whatever distance the handler feels comfortable with, controlled by voice command. Because of this, the officer is able to work at a safer distance when pursuing armed suspects.

— the dog is able to work freely without being restricted by the longe line getting tangled or otherwise hung up. If the dog can be controlled with complete accuracy by voice command, the stress and strain of the line are completely eliminated.

— the officer is able to keep his hands free for his weapon at all times and can send the dog in to attack without having to release the longe line.

— the officer must learn to accurately read his dog's physical signs since he cannot feel the signals he would when working on-line.

— the dog must be a reliable animal which can be instantly controlled by voice in any given situation. Failure on his part to respond instantly could result in his being hit by a vehicle or other such occurrences.

— when a track proceeds through a busy area and the officer loses sight of the dog as he rounds a corner or some obstacle, the continuity of the track is lost. To assure true accuracy the dog must be kept within sight of the handler so that proper track continuity may be given as evidence in court.

— each of the constant commands necessary to hold the dog back for the handler to catch up or to maintain visual contact momentarily distracts the dog. This allows the suspect more time to put distance between himself and the pursuing dog team.

— when the dog is working off-line he will have a tendency to overshoot turns in the track. Much care must be taken to overcome this difficulty.

These are only a few of the advantages and disadvantages to each style of tracking. The decision is yours as to which style you will use. You may find that circumstances also will dictate whether you use on-line or off-line tracking. By combining the best of both in varying circumstances you can obtain very pleasing results.

When working off-lead, utilize the same basic tactics as you did on-lead. The only difference is that when your dog starts working at a distance and you require him to slow down or to wait for you to catch up, you must command him to stay or go down; this breaks his concentration upon the track. However, you will find that once you catch up to your partner and command him to search for the suspect again, he will pick up on the track and continue on very easily. This method of controlling your dog by voice command is easily accomplished if your partner has learned his obedience routines satisfactorily.

Should you encounter specific problems off-lead, revert to on-lead tracking to work out the problem, and each time work an identical track off-lead to show the dog that he must be consistent, whether off-lead or on-lead, to obtain success.

Failure to succeed in off-line tracking often results from poor control over the dog through a lack of proper obedience training.

Area Searches/Sweeps

This section makes extensive use of the dog's olfactory capabilities to pursue airborne scent, combined with the *go right* and *go left* commands. The area sweeps are used to search areas where there may be a lost person or a hiding suspect, but there is no starting point from which to track, or where the length of time since the person was last seen makes it impossible for the dog to track. For example, a child lost in a forest would not be easily tracked by the dog if he or she was missing overnight. Therefore the area where the subject would most likely be found is searched by the dog.

Start out by dropping an article such as a coat in an area of high grass. Leave the area and allow your scent to dissipate. Take the dog to the area and instruct him to *search lost*. Always work downwind of the article so that the airborne scent coming off the coat can be easily picked up by the dog. When he finds the coat, whether or not by accident, praise him and have him retrieve it to you or play a game of tug of war with him.

Place various articles in different locations and continue to work the dog until he understands the command *search lost*. Use progressively smaller articles until your partner is meticulous enough to locate items at least as small as a man's wallet. Your dog's capabilities are limited only by the amount of work you are willing to do with him. Sgt. Rick Fackrell of the London Ontario Police Force once used his partner PSD Prince to search for and successfully locate a diamond ring which had been lost in a snow-bank. The possibilities are endless.

Once your partner is adept at area searching, use various quadrants and send him out by commanding him to *go right* and *search lost*, and so on. Practice in various terrains with different kinds of articles to improve your partner's ability to find items which are buried, hidden and dropped. Coax him to the proper location if necessary and see that he always locates and digs up, retrieves or otherwise indicates the article, even if you have to show him where it is. Make him think it is his success, however, and this will help to build his confidence.

When you hit the streets as a working team you may be required to search alleys for discarded weapons, stolen and discarded purses, money

deposit bags, and so on. You may also be required to search a field for a body or heavy bush for a suspect or lost child. In each circumstance you will have to establish a series of grids so that the areas are properly covered. As your dog covers each area with negative results, go on to the next.

To prepare for various circumstances which may arise, simulate these possibilities in training. One situation that comes to mind is where a police service dog was called in to search a building which had collapsed while under construction. The dog was used to area-search the rubble and to locate bodies and injured survivors. Although this dog was not trained specifically for this purpose, it should be noted that "cadaver dogs" are becoming more common, particularly in areas of high crime and internal strife.

The potential applications of the dogs are restricted only by your imagination. If you as a handler have a full understanding of your partner, you will be capable of handling situations where otherwise lives would be lost. Often these situations are ones in which administrators would not normally think the dogs would be useful, as in the above incident. It is up to you to train your partner to be versatile and to make others aware of his versatility.

Remember also that when you are doing an area search for a suspect or a lost child, you must be able to indicate to your partner whether to attack or to stay and indicate his position. Only a well-trained dog which can be controlled entirely off-lead can be trusted not to attack when it is not warranted and vice versa.

Once your partner has become a consistent tracker through all types of terrain and adverse conditions, the time has come to progress to aggression training. When your dog has learned to threaten and attack on command, the tracking sequences can be implemented into the aggression work. Set up situations where the dog tracks the suspect and at the end of the track confronts the suspect. Once your dog has completed the aggression phase of training, your use of varied exercises with different outcomes is the key to becoming a versatile team.

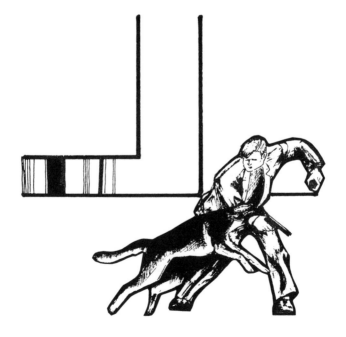

10
Aggression
and Criminal Apprehension

Quarry Selection and Application

The quarry is the most vital link in the training of the police service dog. These quarries should be chosen for their acting ability and physical agility, and must be able to read accurately the actions, reactions, and personality of the PSD.

A quarry should have complete confidence in the handler's abilities. Once recruited, the quarry should make an effort to ride along with a police officer on the street to observe actual situations and suspects, so that he can learn to duplicate them as closely as possible.

The following basics should be strictly adhered to by the quarry:

— Never feed the sleeve to the dog, make him work for it. Make him come to the sleeve.

— Don't appear to be on the defensive or cower into corners in advanced phases of training.

— Constant eye contact should be maintained with the dog to observe the animal's intended attack point. If necessary, take action to avoid a low bite.

— Scream when attacked and increase the screaming as the bite pressure by the K9 increases. Note: *Make sure you maintain his bite on the sleeve. You as the quarry must ensure that the dog wins his battle.*

— Use different buildings, scenes and actions, i.e., building searches, city and rural tracks, simulated pursuits with subsequent car ditching and foot pursuit.

— The dog must win the whole fight. Act as if the sleeve is a real arm.

— Be cautious for caught teeth, don't damage the dog. *If he bites lightly and you get away, run as a suspect would. Do not feed the arm back to him.* Remember also that the harder the arm guard, the harder the dog will learn to bite.

Handlers should take note of the following points:

— For advanced aggression, use the leash through a pivot point and restrain the PSD as the quarry attacks you. Once the dog is sufficiently teased up, fall as if injured, releasing the leash and allowing the dog to take out the quarry. This is also an excellent method for getting the more docile candidates worked up.

— Make sure that the dog escorts the suspect back to the car after each successful attack. The dog should be wary of the culprit until he is properly secured in the rear of the car.

Equipment

Leather collar, fifteen-foot lead, six-foot lead, gunny sack, visible and hidden ballistic arm guards are required.

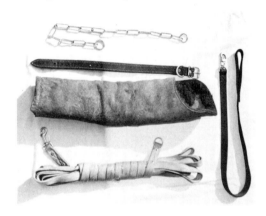

Stage One

Begin the aggression training by playing with the dog and getting him used to holding things in his mouth. Aggression training must be slow and deliberate as up to this point you have taught your partner to be obedient and friendly towards others. He is very trusting in his human friends and therefore has no inclination to attack. We must, through a series of training sequences, teach him that he is required to be aggressive in certain circumstances.

Tug-of-war is a simple, effective way to begin this training. It also fulfils the animal's need for playtime and aids in the dog/handler bonding process.

Using a gunny sack, tease the dog until he snaps or grabs for the sack. Whenever he holds onto the sack, praise him and use the command *take him*. Once his bite on the sack is strong he will start to plant his feet and tug in an attempt to win it from you. Make sure that in the first few instances he wins his battle, but only after you put up a good solid resistance. When he has mastered the game, you can implement the command *out* and make him release his hold on the sack. Never allow him to grab the sack again until you let him know it is O.K. to do so.

Stage Two

To start, place your leash on the dead ring of the choke collar or on the wide leather collar, depending on your personal preference. In my training I use the leather collar extensively for crowd control and to cue the dog that we are going to be doing aggression or "man work." As the training progresses the use of the collar is dropped entirely with the exception of crowd control situations.

Here, we introduce the quarry. He must read your dog so that he knows the instant the dog notices him. As soon as he is noticed, he must make a great show of being fearful and scurry off as if a grizzly bear were on his trail.

Locate an area where the quarry can approach suddenly from different locations. Place your dog in the sit position beside you and have the quarry enter. There should have been no previous contact between you and the quarry within hearing or seeing distance of the dog, to prevent him from knowing you are familiar with the subject.

As the quarry enters, give your dog the command *watch him*. Be excited and attempt to transfer your enthusiasm to him. Your quarry should first enter in a manner which will cause the dog to be suspicious, whether he crooks over or crabs along close to the ground. He may wish to wear a long coat. The idea, of course, is to provoke some kind of reaction in the dog.

When it is apparent that the dog is paying attention to the suspect, the quarry must exit the area giving the impression he is afraid of the dog. It is not necessary for the dog to bark or be otherwise aggressive in the beginning. This will come with time. He need only pay attention to the quarry, watching his every move, ears forward, for the quarry to run in fear. Should he bark or pull at the lead in an attempt to investigate, so much the better.

This stage of training should continue at various times of the day and night. The quarry should very subtly increase his challenge to the dog by getting closer to the animal or waiting for the first whimper, growl or bark before exiting. Maintain the dog's curiosity until he can stand it no longer. Above all, utilize different quarries and make sure there is no contact between the quarry and the dog at the present level of training. Increase the amount of agitation until the dog barks aggressively at the quarry.

Stage Three

Now comes the critical stage at which the quarry must challenge the dog to the point where some type of confrontation takes place. The quarry must be able to read the dog well and must ensure that it wins the battle. There is a need for caution here in that if the challenge is too strong, and the dog backs off or shows fear, you will set your training back; this is why you must increase the levels of aggression very slowly. Should the dog back off at some point, go back one step and rebuild his self-assurance. It is very important that the animal never lose his confidence. It is also up to the handler to transmit his enthusiasm to the dog and to assure his partner that in certain circumstances it is acceptable for him to sink his teeth into certain individuals.

With the dog on a six-foot lead the quarry enters, gunny sack in hand. He should challenge the dog and get him teased into a frenzy, but not let him have the sack. The quarry should work his way to within reach of the dog. All animals have what is commonly known as the flight zone. That is the area between the dog and the intruder in which the dog feels safe and capable of escaping. Once the intruder enters this flight zone the dog either must turn tail and run or he must stand his ground and fight.

The quarry has entered the dog's flight zone and because the handler is holding him there he has no alternative but to stand his ground. In some cases the dog will attempt to hide behind the handler but the quarry should "flank" the dog (i.e., pull the hair of the flanks underneath the rear legs) as soon as he has lost the animal's attention. This serves two purposes: it teaches the dog that he must observe the suspect at all times to prevent being hurt, and it snaps him into the reality that this character cannot be trusted at all.

When the quarry flanks the dog, he will most likely spin around and snap with surprise and pain. The quarry must instantly react in a great show of fear and exit the scene. Repeat this procedure until the dog makes no attempt to back off, and begin to incorporate the gunny sack into the routine by teasing him with it. Again, should the animal ever fail to pay attention to the quarry from this time on, the suspect should "back-sneak" and flank the animal effectively.

Continue to increase the level of aggression until the dog snaps at the quarry. At this point the sack should be flung out for the dog to grab onto. The handler should give the command *stop him* and encourage his partner to attack. As soon as the dog grabs onto the sack, the quarry should make his fearful exit. Note that at each stage the dog wins his battle, even though at first he didn't realize he was having a battle. The quarry has, by careful reading of the dog's behavior, manipulated him into ever-increasing levels of agitation. As the exercises continue, the handler must emphasize control on the dog by making him sit properly and by standing in position without putting strain on the lead during the *watch* commands. The dog should be permitted to lunge forward only when he is given the command *stop him*. At the end of every sequence, when the sack is taken from the dog by the handler, the command *out* should be utilized. This command is similar to a dog's bark and is therefore very effective in getting your partner to listen and obey.

It should be noted that the command *out* is used only to stop the aggression of your partner, never to correct him or to stop him from doing what comes naturally. For example, the command *no* should always be used to correct the dog and let him know he is doing something of which you disapprove. If your dog has attacked a quarry and you wish him to cease his attack the command *out* is given. When my partner is on a track and does something such as sniff traces of another dog's urine on a hydrant, I use the command *phooey*. Each of these three commands fulfils a distinct purpose. To sniff another animal's urine is natural for the dog, and therefore I do not wish to interfere by using the command *no* and giving him the impression it is something which is bad. In his view it is not bad, and in my view it is only inconvenient, so the idea is to let him know that we want him to get back to the task at hand. To use the command *no* is to distinctly tell him he is doing wrong, whereas the command *out* tells him to cease his aggression and is simply an obedience command.

The achieved level of agitation should be repeated vigorously until the dog attacks the sack held by the quarry. A struggle should ensue, with the dog finally pulling the sack away from the quarry, and the quarry fleeing. Praise your dog enthusiastically and remember to utilize the appropriate commands through all levels of agitation.

Stage Four

We now implement the use of the arm guard on the quarry. Various styles of guards are on the market. An easy rule to remember is that the harder the sleeve, the harder the dog learns to bite. The softer the sleeve, the weaker the dog's bite will be.

My own preference for training is the barrel sleeve. This form of arm guard offers no extra T-bar, V-bar or other style of bite bar to assist the dog in holding on. For optimal results, the barrel sleeve is by far the superior guard, as it is the hardest for the dog to get a good bite onto and his bite must be full and firm to maintain a grip on the suspect. The barrel sleeve is also the closest in shape to the human arm, with the exception of the ballistic sleeves which are used under clothing during advanced training.

Have the quarry wear the sleeve and carry the gunny sack into the training area. Give the dog the *watch* command and allow the quarry to work up the dog. Once the dog is ready to attack give him the command *take him* and let the quarry do the rest. The quarry at this point must encourage the dog to be aggressive, so he should retreat a few paces and act fearful before the dog reaches him. As the dog comes forward the quarry should attempt to place the sleeve towards the animal, yet at the same time make the animal work for it. A half-hearted backhand swing in an attempt to hit the dog in the face will usually suffice to obtain the dog's first bite. The quarry should immediately drop the sleeve and run scared, while the handler praises his dog. The point of carrying the gunny sack during this stage of training is that the quarry can wrap it around the sleeve for the dog to attack the first few times if he is leery of biting the sleeve. Again, we have a series of progressions until the dog attacks the quarry and holds on during a formidable struggle, until finally the battle is won and the suspect is defeated. If at any point in the training the dog should leave himself open, turn away from the quarry or fail to attack, the quarry should flank the dog and escape wherever possible. This keeps the dog alert and prevents him from getting his "bite" reward if he fails to perform adequately.

Work the dog until the sack is no longer required to tease him, and he will attack the suspect's arm without any hesitation. If you are experiencing difficulty in getting the dog excited enough to attack, make use of the dog's sense of loyalty to his master. Run the leash around a pivot point (such as a fence post or a flagpole.) With the lead attached to the leather collar and the handler holding firmly from the other end, the quarry can enter and attack the handler. The dog is kept just out of reach of the confrontation and when the animal's intensity of aggression appears high, the handler falls to the ground, releases the dog as he falls and allows his partner the opportunity to come to his rescue. This method is nearly always successful when all else fails.

Stage Five

The dog should be a formidable opponent for the quarry by this point, and various locations, different situations and suspects should be used. This will prevent familiarization with any particular situation or quarry in preparation for attack work.

Work the dog using the dead ring on the collar at all times, with the exception of this lessons sequence. This series of lessons is to encourage maximum control over the dog, and to teach him to *out*, i.e., release the quarry or article, on command.

Go through the same routines with your quarry. He should no longer have to act in an unusual manner as your partner should by now be reacting to your commands. Send your dog in on the attack sequence. When the suspect has been attacked, order the quarry to "freeze." Once his movement has ceased, command your dog *out*. With your lead attached to the choke chain take a firm grip and snap the lead with enough force to out the dog off the suspect. Allow him to continue barking at the suspect, but see that he makes no effort to re-attack when the suspect is motionless. Later in training you will be required to send the dog on an attack after a motionless suspect, but at this point we want him to guard the suspect and attack if the quarry attempts to flee. Set up various situations and work on the *out* command. When the dog starts to come off on his own without prompting with physical correction, praise him thoroughly.

Go through the same routines utilizing the longe line. Set up situations where the quarry runs from the dog and your partner pursues and attacks him. Utilizing the longe on the choke collar, you can call *out* from your distant position and still maintain control by correcting him sharply if he fails to comply. Continue this training until your partner will cease his aggressive moves immediately on command.

Stage Six

Your partner must be able to cease his movements of aggression even prior to attacks in certain situations, for example, where an unarmed suspect surrenders and there is no danger of further aggressive activity. Other circumstances, such as a change in situation, may arise. You may find, for example, that you have just sent your partner on an attack against a person who appears to be fleeing the scene of a crime when in fact he is the property owner chasing the real suspects. Recently an officer in Washington State tracked a suspect from a violent domestic assault. As the dog closed in he was sent on an attack to take down the still-fleeing suspect when the dog handler was informed via his portable radio that the victim of the assault had withdrawn the complaint and refused to file charges. This officer had a well-trained partner and was able to call the dog off just as the dog jumped to attack the suspect.

This kind of control shows your level of expertise and can prevent lawsuits in many circumstances. It is essential that you strive for this level of control of your partner. Proper obedience and signal control training provide you with an excellent base from which to work. This is the reason we stress the obedience sections prior to any aggression training.

Repeat the training sessions as previously noted, utilizing the longe line attached to the active ring on the choke collar. Ensure that your partner is corrected sharply should he pull on the lead at all. You should never have to strain to hold your dog back and he must learn that he must not attack unless directed to do so, either through your direct command or through the aggressive actions of the suspect. When he is required to attack he will have full freedom to work and need not fear any correction unless he fails to comply with your *out* command.

Have the quarry enter, and send the dog on the attack using the command *take him*. As the dog leaves your side the quarry stops dead in his tracks and is no longer acting as a threat. Call your dog loudly and sharply, giving him the command *out*. Should he fail to comply, turn around and with the end of your longe line run in the opposite direction until your dog comes to the end of the line. Repeat the command *out* just prior to jerking him off his feet.

Intersperse this procedure with the routine of letting the dog attack and struggle with the suspect, and then calling him off after he has his bite. He must learn to cease his aggressive movements on command instantly. Continue setting up various situations until you are confident you can call the dog out in any situation, even from a full run. Any failure on the part of your partner to comply should be met instantly with severe choke chain correction, and proper results should be met with excited praise. Keep the emphasis on control at all times. Utilize the same corrective procedures with the six-foot lead if your partner fails to cease attacking the quarry on your command. Simply jerk him off his feet with such force that he will not wish to repeat the experience.

For those of you with overzealous partners who have difficulty in yanking your dog off the quarry's arm, try pulling the collar sharply downward and towards the quarry. At the same time have the quarry force his arm further into the dog's mouth. This combined action causes the same physical discomfort to the dog as the previous corrections and causes the dog's jaws to be forced uncomfortably wide open to the point of causing a gag reflex. This combination is usually sufficient to gain a successful release of the quarry. After repeated sequences your partner should be releasing smoothly on command. After every command *out*, the dog should be encouraged to watch the suspect closely. In the beginning you may find it necessary to give him the command *watch him*, but he will soon learn to keep an eye on the suspect automatically.

Stage Seven

We must now implement the use of the ballistic sleeve, with the quarry wearing a shirt or jacket overtop, giving the impression that there is no arm guard. Up to this point it has been merely a game to the dog, and quite often it takes some work to get him to bite what he thinks is an unprotected arm.

The quarry should be supplied with a short, narrow length of bamboo cane for this exercise. During the attack phases he can use it to swat the dog across the buttocks a few times. This reinforces the dog's mistrust of anyone whom his master indicates is suspect, and also teaches him to withstand pain. I am not in favor of striking dogs, but during this sequence the odd switch will help prepare the dog for the far more formidable weapons encountered on the street. My own partner was once struck with a metal bar right across the snout, but he maintained his bite on the subject to a successful takedown. You cannot afford to have a partner who will back off if attacked. It is dangerous for you and for him.

Once the quarry has prepared himself with the hidden arm and switch, have him enter the area suddenly and attack. As in the previous sequences send the dog in to apprehend, and allow the suspect to use the switch on him a few times. Now when you order the suspect to freeze and you call your dog out, command him to stay while you approach the suspect and remove the weapon. A longe line can be attached to the dog's choke collar and run back to a second hidden trainer, who can pull on the lead effectively should your partner break his position while you are searching the suspect. If you are without a second trainer and your dog attacks while you are doing your search, call him out, and utilizing much force on his choke chain, drag him back to the original position in which you placed him when you told him to stay.

Advance this training using a revolver or pistol loaded with blank ammunition. The quarry advances firing into the air and continues to do so as the dog attacks and holds. Again go through the *out, stay,* and *search* routines. After each encounter place your dog at heel and allow him to escort his prisoner back to the police cruiser. Make certain that he continues

to pay attention until the suspect is placed into the car with the doors closed. Only then should the dog be permitted to relax.

Repeat the sequences in this stage until you can send the dog on the attack and call him out at any stage of the proceedings. Work on the search and escort routines until you know you have complete control over your partner and he can be trusted to guard the suspect without attacking as you search him.

Stage Eight

Start to use variations and perform various exercises. Equip the quarry with the ballistic sleeve covered by a shirt or jacket and have him wear the visible arm guard on the other arm. When the exercise begins, the quarry enters the area and attacks the dog, running straight towards him screaming. The dog is sent on the attack by the handler and the quarry positions himself so the dog attacks the visible sleeve. After a good struggle the quarry drops the visible sleeve and runs in an attempt to escape. The dog should drop the sleeve immediately and pursue the quarry, attacking him again.

The training can include various combinations including multiple suspects, quarry attacking while firing a gun, and pursuing a suspect who has shucked an arm guard after being attacked. Throughout all stages of this training the dog should never be allowed to become "sack-happy." His attention should be on the quarry at all times. Even if the dog has successfully removed the sleeve from the quarry he should drop it and immediately redirect his attention to the quarry.

The quarries should continue to increase their level of aggression until the dog is fearless of being attacked by a suspect firing a gun and/or striking him with a switch.

On all weapons training, the weapon should be held in the arm which is contained in the sleeve. Once the quarry is attacked he should drop his weapon and submit to the dog.

Harass and Delay Tactics

The use of harass and delay tactics as opposed to straight attack sequences against suspects is simply a matter of personal preference. The harass and delay procedure is used extensively in Germany by customs agents who work dogs on free tracks in bush areas. Suspects engaged in smuggling activities learned to defeat the dogs by wearing a protective arm guard. When the dogs searched out the culprits and attacked, usually working at a distance from the handler through heavy bush, the suspect would offer the protected arm which the dog would take. The suspect would then stab the dog with a knife and be well clear of the scene long before the handler was able to locate his fatally-injured partner. The method was silent and effective until the agency started to train the dogs in harass and delay techniques.

This technique consists of the dog locating the suspect and circling him. At the same time he voices his position to the handler by continual barking and does not attack until directed to do so.

For my purposes I prefer the direct approach. As a team, my partner and I normally work within close range of one another. Should we encounter a suspect whom I consider to be a potential danger, the dog is sent to attack immediately. His purpose is to eliminate any risk which that suspect may represent to me or to others. Whether the suspect is advancing to confront me, running away in a bid to escape, sitting in a chair or lying on a bed, the dog will attack without hesitation when sent to do so.

You will have occasion to enter homes or rooms containing a known felon and although he may not be armed, he may have weapons within reach. If the subject is known to have a violent history, is armed or if I observe a weapon within his reach, the dog is sent to attack instantly before the culprit has any opportunity to arm himself.

I fully endorse training your dog to attack subjects who are sitting, lying down or standing perfectly still. Suspects have been known to remain perfectly still to keep the dog from attacking. When the handler then approaches, the suspect suddenly produces a firearm and a potentially fatal confrontation develops. The proper deployment of the dog on a suspect who is armed or believed to be armed must be swift and sure, no matter what the efforts of the culprit to avoid attack. Any hesitation on the part of the dog could have fatal consequences.

Weapons Avoidance

For advanced training, as the dog holds onto the quarry's arm, the quarry can use his free hand and slap the dog across the side of the face, while turning his body slowly in the direction of the attacked arm. For example, if the dog is holding the left arm, the quarry, using his right hand, should slap the dog across the left side of his face and at the same time turn counter-clockwise. If the dog is on the right arm, slap him with the left hand and turn clockwise. The dog eventually learns to turn automatically in the direction of the arm to prevent being slapped, and eventually learns to swing the suspect in a circle. This effectively prevents the suspect from gaining any degree of control of the situation and makes it very difficult for him to strike the dog or use any weapon against him.

Prisoner Search and Escort

At the conclusion of every successful apprehension the dog should be instructed to come to a heel next to the handler. As the handler prepares to search the quarry, the dog should be left at a sit-stay position directly behind the suspect. Proper searching procedures should be implemented and the culprit then escorted by the dog and handler to the nearest patrol car. Exercises should be done which teach the dog to stay in position watching the quarry unless the handler is attacked or the quarry flees. In both cases the dog should be taught to attack immediately without verbal commands. However, should the dog attempt to attack the suspect when in fact the suspect takes no action, he should be corrected instantly.

Vehicle Exit/Handler Protection

Each dog car is built in such a manner that the separator between the front and rear compartment can be left open for the dog to jump into the front seat. A series of exercises should be executed in which the dog is called out of the car by the handler. Both sides of the car should be used so that the dog is accustomed to exiting from either the driver or the passenger side of the vehicle. The reason for this is that in high-traffic areas it may be preferable to leave the driver's side window rolled up and the passenger window down so that the dog does not exit directly into heavy traffic. Set up "traffic stop" situations where the handler is suddenly attacked by the quarry. Work the dog until he is confident in exiting the vehicle through the cage and out either side without hesitation.

Crowd Control

Dogs can be effective visual deterrents in crowd problem situations. However, using them to control unruly crowds by the use of indiscriminate attack work is unwarranted and a dangerous practice. If required to make a break in a crowd in order to rescue a fallen officer, or to act as backup in an emergency, or to guard the police vehicles, the dog's use is warranted. In most cases, simply having the dogs visible and ready to go is deterrent enough. In any case it is up to the officer in charge as to how you deploy your partner in such situations. As the dog handler, however, you have the final decision as to how to deploy the dog. Use that choice wisely and with much discretion, particularly in cases which involve potential crowd violence.

Once your dog is doing well, you may wish to implement some crowd control work with him. This is done quite simply with the use of multiple

quarries of which one or two may be equipped with hidden ballistic sleeves. To work the dog on a large group, send him out on the longe line with the *watch him* command. Anyone who comes within range of his teeth is fair game. Instruct your quarries to come in from the crowd periodically to allow the dog his bites. Another variation to this training is to have the crowd surround you in a large circle. With the dog on the longe line have the quarries come within range from different angles. Allow the dog to attack in one direction, and call him out when you see another suspect enter the designated zone. This is one example in which the use of the *out* command is vital in order to rapidly divert his efforts in a new direction. Quickly redirect his attention to the new offender and send him on the attack. Allow him to work at the length of the line if necessary to keep the crowd back, but if at all possible keep him close to your side if you are circled, as it will take him less time to span the radius of the circle from you to an advancing culprit than if he must cross the entire diameter from one side to the other.

Vehicle Protection

Vehicle protection can be taught along with the aggression training, making use of the same basic routines. The quarry should tease the dog into a frenzy, backing off and letting the dog win repeatedly until ultimately the quarry is bitten by the dog as he tries to enter the vehicle or put his arm in. The handler should be out of sight during this training but close enough to praise the dog when the training is successful.

CAUTION — During all phases of training involving the dog unit and while working the streets, beware of the distance the rear compartment windows are rolled down. Windows which are left open two to three inches risk the possibility of the dog catching his upper front teeth on the top of the window. Subsequent struggles to release himself will result in extensive and painful injury to the dog's teeth, particularly his upper canines. Ensure that the window is rolled sufficiently up or down that there is no danger of your partner getting caught.

Securing of Evidence

Once you have reached an advance stage of aggression and control with your partner, you can train him to watch over evidence or secure a doorway to preserve a crime scene. Place your dog in a down-stay position and situate him in a doorway or place an article between his front legs.

Send in the quarry to attempt to take the article, and observe from a distance. Command your partner verbally to stay in the down position if he breaks. Go through the routine until he realizes that he is on a long down and is to prevent passage or protect the placed article. Teach him that he cannot leave his position to chase after the culprit; he must stay there until the suspect is within reach, rather than working towards the offender. When he attacks he must *out* once the offender backs off and should return to his position beside the article he is protecting. Again it is simply a series of progressions and numerous situation setups. You must be patient and careful not to confuse your partner, so take your time.

Once he has completed his training you will be able to use him to secure buildings, apprehend fleeing suspects, work crowd control, or secure pieces of evidence. Work your dog thoroughly and place your emphasis on control; it is the key to precise work in any phase of training.

Mailman-Milkman Theory

This section is intended to clear up the mystery of why so many family pets turn from lovable balls of fur into vicious monsters who seem to live for nothing more than making a meal out of your local delivery person. I hope that some hints I include will also help to reduce the number of injuries these service people incur in the course of their work.

Simply stated, these courageous individuals have, without realizing what they are doing, gradually attack-trained your family pet. Any pet with any amount of curiosity and spunk can become quite a formidable protection dog if properly trained. By the same token, it can be trained by the mailman, milkman, or any other service person to be a formidable opponent without any knowledge on the part of the "trainer" that this is actually occurring.

Reviewing the steps of aggression training discussed earlier in this chapter, the quarry approaches the dog, the dog demonstrates curiosity and suddenly the quarry runs away screaming fearfully. Over a period of time, more stress is put on the dog by the quarry until he barks once, lunges, or even growls, and then again, the quarry leaves the scene. This progression continues until finally the dog is growling, barking and snapping, wanting nothing more than to attack the quarry. Suddenly the quarry returns, the opportunity finally arises and the dog attacks. The dog has successfully been trained as an attack dog. He has learned that if he stands his ground, he can win every battle.

Now, compare what occurs with your delivery person every day. He or she walks up your driveway to the front door. The family pet, hearing someone coming, goes to the door to investigate. The mailman opens the mailbox and drops the letters through the slot into the house where they fall down in front of your watchful pet. Upon closer investigation by your pet, the mailman lets go of the mail slot, whether in the door or on the outside wall, it clatters shut and he turns and walks away. This eventually sets a pattern for the dog. Every day this fellow walks up to the door and the dog goes to investigate; the dog learns to anticipate his coming, gets to the door, and becoming braver each time, starts to bark. Of course the "suspect" mailman leaves immediately.

This progression continues until we have simply another dog that has been trained, by a mailman or milkman who has unwittingly acted as the ideal quarry, to protect his property. This is a difficult problem to correct if your pet is already accustomed to aggressive behavior towards delivery people. However, the family that honestly cares about its relationship with these service people, and especially those families with a new pet, should ask the regular delivery or service person to attempt to get acquainted with the pet. He should take the time to pet him, talk to him, throw his ball a few times and play with him in an effort to show the dog that he is not leaving because he is afraid. The service person should be confident and should leave only when he is ready to, not as soon as the dog pays attention to him.

If the delivery person spends just a few minutes each day with the animals on his route, he will find some dramatic changes in just a few weeks. In fact, the dog may look forward to the visits rather than being antagonistic. A good example of this occurred with one of my own dogs. Our milkman was fearful of our dogs and particularly of German Shepherds because of a previous incident in which he had been attacked. Over a period of time the dog came to sense his hesitation and fear, and although he had never done so in the past, started to growl at him. It was not long before the barking started, and the dog became more and more aggressive towards this particular serviceman. I was unable to convince the man to take the time to get to know the dog, although I had tried to explain why he was getting these reactions from the dog. Shortly thereafter a new man took over the route. Whenever he came to do a delivery he showed confidence, speaking to the dog as he approached, greeting him with some excitement, as if he was well-known to the dog. He took the time to visit, and on occasion would pour a damaged carton of milk into the dog's food bowl. These two delivery people had entirely different approaches, and received entirely different reactions from my Shepherd.

It is very difficult for a serviceman not to fear most dogs, as during his career he has likely been attacked, and to say the least, he probably has not reaped much satisfaction from the outcome! Consequently a mailman, when confronted by a dog, will on most occasions emit a fear scent from his sweat glands, and will naturally be more cautious. This tells the dog that this individual may be an easy mark, which increases his level of aggression accordingly. Dogs will often test a person until they know they have the upper hand, and then will suddenly attack.

There is no sure method for circumventing this problem, but there are certain evasive moves which the person confronted by such a dog can implement. Should you find yourself in such a situation, you should first of all stay calm and try to avoid becoming fearful. This will help in controlling the fear scent released from your body. By ignoring the dog and continuing on, you are also showing confidence without aggression, and are not giving in to his tests. If he continues and you are trapped, turn slowly sideways, kneel down, and avoid looking directly at him. From his instinctive point of view you are being submissive to him; in most cases the dog will cease his aggressive action. Confronting the dog while standing tall will likely bring on an attack because you are putting yourself inside the dog's flight zone and threatening him. Above all, remain calm and avoid being aggressive or even appearing aggressive in any way. If this flight zone is maintained it is probable that you will be able to back away from a potentially dangerous situation.

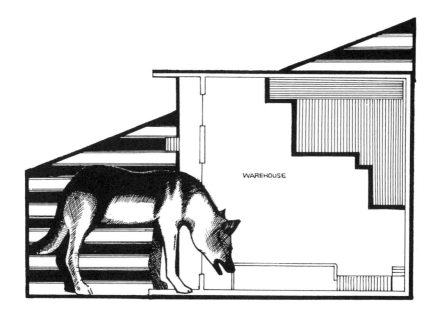

WAREHOUSE

11
Building Searches

Building searches for suspects involved in robberies or burglaries are becoming more common. More often than not, these searches take place at night and involve culprits who have been contained within a building by patrol members who either answered a silent alarm or happened on the burglary in progress.

Various difficulties will arise when using dogs for these searches, and these are largely unrelated to the actual ability of the dog to sense and indicate the suspects. Most of the problems involve the animal's footing and his ability to adjust to unusual surroundings.

Before you start training for building searches, you should study the type of community in which you work and identify various factories, schools, warehouses and stores to which you may be called. Arrangements should be made with the managers or proprietors to gain access to the facilities during off hours for training.

Stage One

Before the actual search training begins, the dog should be taken to these buildings and allowed to wander through them. Slippery tile floors are one of the most difficult surfaces for the dog to become accustomed to. He will have a tendency to extend his claws in an effort to grasp onto the surface. This only makes it harder for him to maintain control, and he will sprawl out and slide around until he realizes he has better footing with his claws retracted. Another exercise which demonstrates this is the barrel pyramid hurdle of the obstacle course. The enamel paint on the barrels forms a slick surface and the dog must learn to keep his claws withdrawn in order to scale the hurdle more easily.

The dog should also be familiarized with buildings which have catwalks or high lofts, stairs or short industrial ladders. One surface which is commonly problematic for dogs is the transparent catwalk, made with metal mesh. As a part of the dog's basic training, he should be familiarized with all of these various types of floor surfaces as well as with sources of loud and unusual industrial noise so that he will adjust easily to changes in surface and to the stress of unusual surroundings. Once he has learned to be relaxed in all types of situations, the actual search training may begin.

143

Building-search training is very similar to track training in that you entice the dog by the use of a quarry. Again, each stage of training is a progression which builds the dog's confidence. Once the dog is familiar with various buildings, agitation work should be done inside each area, with the quarry using the concealed sleeve. Carry on attack work on the stairs, hallways and numerous rooms until the dog is prepared to take on the suspect in any location. Include training in the cellblock and booking areas of your station. Have the quarry tease the dog, then run and hide around the corner, inside a closet or up high on a shelf. After a minute or two has passed, send the dog and give him the command *find him*. Once the dog finds the suspect, encourage him to bark. This is a must when doing building searches. If the dog has trouble locating the quarry, have the suspect hiss or make some sort of noise to assist the dog in making the location. Agitate the dog until he is barking continuously and giving positive indications before you allow the quarry into a position where your partner can be rewarded with a bite.

Stage Two

Our next step is to have the agitator work on the dog outside the building with the handler holding the dog back. Once the dog is adequately agitated, have the quarry run into the building and allow him time to hide. Follow the same procedures as outlined previously and encourage the dog to bark when he locates the suspect. During this exercise the outside doors should be left open; make certain that the dog watches the quarry enter the building.

Note: Quarries must be constantly changed in this and any other agitation exercise to prevent familiarity to the dog.

Stage Three

This time the dog is not pre-agitated, nor does he see the quarry enter the building. The agitator hides in a closed location before the handler and dog enter the area. When starting out, there should be a short time delay before the team's entry into the building, with this delay increasing as the dog becomes more confident in his abilities.

On arrival, cue the dog and give him the command to search the building. During these first few times it would assist the dog to start the search from the same point where the quarry entered the building. Again, follow through with the proper indications, encouraging him to bark and praising him on his find. Allow him his bites, intermingled sporadically with successful searches in which he must escort the suspect back to the car without achieving a bite. Repeat each exercise until the dog is successful on every occasion before going on to the next stage.

Stage Four

Repeat the previous stage, but prolong the time delay and include two suspects hiding at different locations within the building. Once he has located the first suspect, have the suspect removed, then continue on to the next suspect. Increase the time delays between the time the quarry hides and the time the dog is brought into action. Continue the training using multiple suspects, various locations, searches resulting in bites and escorts, as well as searches without bites. Hide the quarries in high locations and practice in buildings with air conditioning on and off.

On the Street

While this book was being written, two police officers were fatally wounded in two separate incidents. Each officer was investigating a burglary in progress. These tragedies are becoming more common in Canada and the United States and we must utilize more caution than ever on the streets. As K9 officers you will be more involved in direct contact with dangerous criminals than any other person in the law enforcement field. Take advantage of your patrol members. Be sure to take one member with you into the building to act as your cover. Utilize this same tactic when doing open tracks. When you are concentrating on your dog you will not be able to react to danger as quickly as a backup officer who is there specifically for that purpose.

Prior to sending the dog into any building, shout a loud warning to allow the suspects to give themselves up and, more important, to warn any janitors, late-night workers, or other persons who may be inside legitimately to identify themselves and leave the area safely. This can prevent unnecessary bites and possible lawsuits. Make sure the warnings are loud, your instructions clear and that you properly identify yourself.

Make maximum use of light control in all situations. Where advantageous, turn on the lights in the building. Use high-power flashlights rather than the standard triple-cell lights for maximum control of an area.

Shut off the air conditioning whenever possible to prevent the air currents from carrying scents which will result in false indications by your partner. The noise from the heating or air conditioning units can also prevent you and your dog from hearing suspects which may be close by.

Even in buildings where the heating and air conditioning systems are off, there is the phenomenon known as the "chimney effect" (discussed also in Chapter 9). This is where a suspect hides in a relatively small or medium-size room. If the room is particularly cool, the suspect's scent will rise to the ceiling, travel across the room, and fall directly opposite the side of the room where the suspect is hiding. Although this does not happen frequently, keep it in mind if the dog remains "hot" in a specific area where you are sure there is no suspect. He is likely directly opposite from where your dog is indicating.

When working with a patrol officer as backup, maintain your distance and utilize all the caution a regular street officer would if he were searching the building without the assistance of a K9 team. The dog is not infallible and there is always the danger that he may pass by the suspect, thereby exposing you to imminent danger.

When working in buildings under construction or which are open to the outside, control over your dog becomes crucial. Beware of open pits, open floors, broken glass, and low walls which your partner may jump and suddenly find that he is two or three stories up.

Beware of rat poisons which may be within the building. Should you see your partner pick up anything in his mouth it should be removed immediately.

Cover your dog as you would any partner. He is just as likely to be assaulted by a suspect with a crowbar as you are. When he has located the suspect in the building, make sure the culprit is searched before being removed from the building.

12

12
Training Exercises

This chapter will help you to develop the standard of performance in your animal necessary for your particular purposes. The idea is to achieve higher levels of control over your partner in given situations and to support your basic training with exercises directed at specific problems you may encounter.

Obedience

Problems which occur during many advanced phases of training stem from a poor level of control over your dog. For total reliability from your partner in exigent situations, you require immediate and positive responses. The basics of obedience are therefore necessary to instill a firm foundation on which to build.

Throughout your basic training, repeat each exercise until the dog shows confidence and skill with each movement. As you proceed through the many weeks of training always repeat the lessons you have completed in the previous weeks to reinforce your partner's proficiency. When you complete a phase of training, continue to use his new talents in varying exercises. This will keep his abilities keen, and as your competence as a team increases you will be able to depend on your partner in critical situations.

Exercises which reinforce the basic obedience training should be directed at your particular needs. For the active jogger, exercises should revolve around situations which you will encounter. For example, work your partner on inside and outside turns, and see that he maintains his close position to you not just at a walking pace but also at a continual run.

If you are a woman training your dog as a jogging companion and personal protector, an excellent idea is the use of saddlebags strapped to your dog's back which would hold any personal items you may require. This eliminates the inconvenience of carrying identification, cash in a wallet or other such items on your person when you are wearing a jogging suit. Besides, what better protection for your personal property than an attack-trained dog who is carrying it in his knapsack? Any mugger with an ounce of common sense is bound to look elsewhere.

Such knapsacks can be homemade with ease, using a standard tracking harness for the basic design. Simply attach satchels of your choice to the harness using straps with Velcro closures which are sewn into the back of each satchel. You can then start exercising your companion while he is wearing the harness. Place it on him with the bags empty and work through a few obedience routines. When he seems to be comfortable with it you can start placing a few articles in the satchels. Remember, he is not a pack horse and it is not necessary to load him down with great amounts of weight; the idea is to give you the simple convenience of having a few personal items with you which are difficult to carry when jogging. Keep the weight light and as evenly distributed as possible. The dog must be able to run alongside you without restriction or added effort and be capable of protecting you aggressively.

As a jogger, one exercise you should work on extensively at various walking and running paces is the *heel*. Work in areas of high traffic and get your partner accustomed to its movement. It is very important that he stop instantly when you stop and that his heel position next to you be very precise at all times. Do your exercises entirely on leash and use heavy corrections until he stops instantly every time you stop. You want to make certain that he never continues on into traffic when you stop at an intersection. When you are sure you can depend on verbal control only to keep your partner in line, remove the leash and work off-lead. Once you have completed aggression training and you have begun your jogging routine, implement the use of quarries along your jogging route to simulate an attack on you as you jog along. Work on your partner's aggression level until he is controllable and easy to call out. Do a series of attacks with the dog wearing the satchels as well.

To prevent potential mishaps, situations with other joggers who jog toward you or pass you from behind should be included in the training, so that your partner learns that these people are not dangerous to you. He should attack only when you are attacked directly.

Distractions

Throughout your obedience training, encourage your partner to work in circumstances involving numerous distractions. Begin with simple problems such as a child throwing a ball into the path of the dog as he works. Vary the kinds of distractions used, to train for the unique circumstances in which you may be required to work as a team. Introduce other dogs into the training area, and bring the odd cat into your training sequence as well until you know your partner will pay strict attention to you and will not be tempted to chase another animal or bolt from whatever task is at hand. Another sequence I like to use is to work a track through a field of cattle or horses, particularly if I'm training a dog for use primarily in a rural area.

Obstacles

Study the area in which you will be working and locate any unusual obstacles you may encounter. Fire escape stairwells, mesh catwalks, picket fences, hedges and chain-link fences are just a few of the more common obstacles which may cause some difficulty for your partner.

You may encounter other problems in specialized work. For example, dogs working search-and-rescue details must be capable of entering and exiting helicopters without hesitation or fear. A dog under stress because of unfamiliar surroundings will not perform with the confidence or consistency needed for the task at hand. The idea is to practice in situations which are common to your specific tasks.

A typical situation your dog may encounter if he is being trained as a drug or bomb dog is that of working in confined spaces such as the cargo area of large aircraft or the underside of vehicles. Some animals find such work very awkward and may try to circumvent the problem. To overcome any aversion the dog may have to working in enclosed or awkward spaces, you must implement the use of obstacles which duplicate his future working situations. Low-built tunnels or crawl spaces, for example, will help your dog to prepare for working under vehicles during drug searches. As you work towards your goals, utilize the underside of various types of vehicles for training situations, or make arrangements with your local airlines to train in aircraft which are down for maintenance work. Officers working in port cities and railway police should also make efforts to train extensively on cargo or passenger ships and through passenger-line train compartments.

Street Survival

As mentioned previously, due to the nature of their work K9 officers are more likely to be involved in armed confrontations than are any other members of the law enforcement team. For this reason I always recommend the use of an escort officer who acts as a backup. When setting up tracking situations, attempt to have a backup officer stay with you so your dog becomes used to the procedure. When the quarry is located, have the backup officer do the physical search of the suspect, handcuff him and remove him. If a second suspect is indicated, the dog handler should wait until the first suspect has been fully secured and the escort officer has returned before proceeding on.

Set up numerous situations, including ambushes, in order to observe your dog's reactions. In some circumstances you will prefer your dog to attack instantly, whereas in others you will want both dog and handler to go to ground instantly. For example, should you be fired upon with a rifle while the suspect is still quite a distance away, it is futile to send the dog on a straight-in attack. Instantaneous use of concealment is quite often the only chance you have for survival. In such circumstances you and your dog must go to ground at once. Work sequences where your dog will simply drop in his tracks when ordered to do so. Remember, however, that concealment is not cover. You may not be visible in high grass or though a wall, but unless you are next to a large boulder or the wall is impenetrable by rifle fire, you are still in trouble.

Once you have taken the only possible action open to you at that point, the next step is to get behind proper cover. If you crawl towards cover in an attempt to get out of the kill zone, and your dog simply walks alongside you, he not only risks being shot himself but is also giving away your position and movement. There are two routines you can use here. First, leave the dog in a down-stay position and crawl to cover yourself. Once behind cover, you may be able to return fire and keep the suspect pinned down while you call your dog to your side. You may also choose to leave the dog in the down position, hoping he is concealed well enough to avoid being shot until more backup arrives and the incident is concluded.

The second approach, which is my personal preference, is to drop to the ground for initial concealment and then crawl to the nearest cover with my partner crawling on his belly beside me. This affords some minimal protection if the dog is between you and the gunfire, and if done properly will not give away your position any more readily than you would crawling along. This also gets the dog out of the kill zone at the same time, affording you the opportunity to reassess your situation and redeploy the dog if necessary.

Adjustable platforms which gradually reduce in height and are wide enough for you and the dog to crawl through together may be used for training. Use the command *creep* or *crawl* and coax him under the obstacle with you. Go slow and easy until he is confident with the unusual movement. An easy obstacle to build for this training is two sheets of plywood which can be mounted end to end on short posts mounted in the ground. Cut grooves at two-inch intervals into the posts so that the plywood can be slipped into the grooves at varying heights. Start your training with the platform positioned at thirty inches in height. Gradually reduce the height of the platform until you are forced to crawl through on your belly and your dog is able to stay by your side. Once your partner is confident and understands the command *creep* or *crawl*, slowly increase the height of the platform but continue encouraging the dog to crawl alongside you. Continue raising the platform until you have it at full height and then work the dog entirely in the open. Should he relapse in his training, simply return to the use of the platform until he performs the exercise flawlessly.

Another duty for which I train every dog is the retrieval of dropped firearms. This sequence can be used should you be involved in a firefight (gun battle) where you drop your sidearm when vaulting over a wall for cover, or are injured and have dropped your weapon out of reach or into an area which affords little or no cover.

Whether you carry a .357 magnum with a six-inch barrel or a .38

special with a four-inch barrel, your partner should be capable of retrieving your weapon to you without difficulty. Some dogs have a difficult time with the heavier weight of the larger-calibre firearms. If the dog is unable to get a grip on the wooden stocks of the weapon he will sometimes be hesitant to pick it up by the metal portions. Continual practice is the key to success, and although not frequently used on the street, this extra bit of training may mean the difference between life and death during a firefight.

Vehicle Exits

In Chapter Seven the advantages and disadvantages of different styles of compartment separators are discussed. Whatever style of compartment you have chosen, make sure your partner is familiar with the proper exit routes. For those units equipped with the opening directly behind the driver, set up situations such as the quarry aggressively attacking you as you sit in the car, or running suspect situations where you suddenly stop the patrol car and lean forward for the dog to do an immediate exit and take-down of the escaping suspect.

Set up car-stop situations where your partner must pay close attention to you at all times. It is very important that you refrain from making every situation one in which the dog must act aggressively. He must learn that not every subject you deal with is dangerous, but at the same time he must remain alert and ready to act in any situation. A dog that watches his partner approach a vehicle and then lies down again in the rear of the patrol unit is of little use in an emergency.

Set up situations that will keep your partner alert at all times. For example, in a scenario in which you are attacked directly by the driver of the checked vehicle and a great fuss occurs, you must also teach the dog to keep a watchful eye out for any indication of handguns or other weapons. Should the suspect suddenly start to point and fire, the dog should instantly react without the need for verbal commands. Work the dog with verbal commands until he has cued in to the various types of circumstances. Gradually reduce the amount of verbal encouragement required until you are confident your partner is always paying close attention to you and will act flawlessly when needed. Anytime it would appear your partner is not paying attention, that is the chance to throw in a twist. It is very important that he remain a vigilant partner at all times.

13

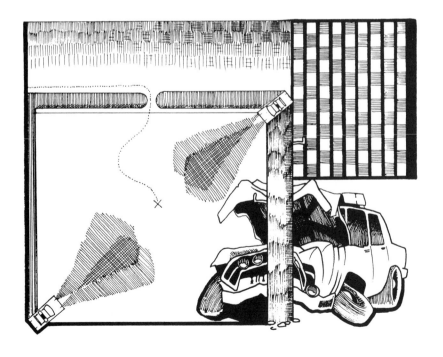

13
Guideline
for Patrol Members

This guideline is meant to assist patrol members in deciding whether to apply a K9 team to a particular situation. For those who know little of the dog's capabilities, it is also intended to aid in the evaluation of situations and deployment of units for proper containment. Finally, this section aims to correct any misconceptions members may have about the capabilities of a police service dog.

The use of this guideline by members of the patrol division will help to increase the number of successful arrests and evidence or property recoveries in cases involving the PSD. The dog is a tool for you to use and the handler is a specialist in his field. Together they are a team that is ready for use at your discretion. However, the best dog-and-handler team in the nation is useless without the proper deployment and assistance of patrol. Too often members of the force contaminate the scene and leave the area soon after the dog team arrives and should the subsequent PSD investigation be inconclusive, incompetence on the part of the dog team is suggested. The use of the K9 unit is a team effort and this cannot be stressed enough. Proper containment by patrol and prompt scene preservation can increase a PSD team's success rate by thirty to forty percent.

When a man and dog team is put together, each must study the other to learn his partner's cues, quirks and behavior. The man is, in fact, the one who does the majority of the learning during training. The dog in his natural state knows how to do everything that is required of him. He knows how to use his nose to track and search. He knows how to retrieve and how to perceive and react to danger. All aspects of the PSD training utilize these natural instincts. The goal is to teach the handler how to get the dog to utilize specific parts of that instinct when it is needed.

Theory of Scent

This section will assist members to understand how to properly contain an area, depending on the individual situation.

To understand why we need containment, patrol members should have an idea of how the dog works on scent. Scent can be broadly divided into

three basic categories:
1. Tunnel or windborne scent.
2. Ground scent.
3. Contact scent.

Tunnel Scent

Tunnel or windborne scent is the scent which is left airborne behind an individual as he walks through a particular area. As he proceeds the scent falls in a cone-like formation around him and drifts in the air, leaving a "tunnel" of identifiable scent wherever the suspect has walked. Windborne scent can also originate from an object dropped by a suspect; this scent may be the result of previous human contact or may be characteristic of the object itself. For example, a scent of leather in the breeze over a grass field will attract the dog's attention as it is a foreign scent, and may subsequently lead the handler to a discarded purse.

Human scent varies according to race, health, cleanliness, nourishment, and amount of physical exertion. The use of the dog's sense of smell upon tunnel and windborne scent depends on body exposure to the prevailing winds. The amount of scent available also depends upon the terrain and wind velocity. It is this type of scenting which is utilized in an area search and which has the most potential for urban areas. The more quickly the dog can be brought to the scent, the greater the chance of apprehension. *Time is the most important factor here, as tunnel scent may dissipate quickly through breezes or evaporation. Urban areas consist mostly of hard surfaces which make contact-scenting difficult. This is why quick response is essential to making use of the available tunnel scent before it dissipates.*

Ground Scent

Ground scent is that which is left by the slightest movement or disturbance. A crushed insect or patch of vegetation leaves particles of moisture on the ground, all of which give off scents, thus indicating a trail. This scent is utilized when tunnel scent is too dissipated to be useful, but is a harder scent to track. As the dog closes in on the suspect, however, he will be able to detect the tunnel scent and you will note his pace quickens as the trail becomes easier to follow.

Contact Scent

This utilizes the theory of transfer discussed in Chapter 9, in which scents are transferred from one area to the next along the track in much the same way that physical traces are transferred by fingerprints onto glass.

Education of patrol members is extremely important for successful police dog work. No one must tramp through an area if the PSD is on the way. The freshest scent in the area will be most readily picked up, and the dog may become confused by the numerous trails. He will pick up trails made by well-meaning but uneducated officers "assisting" to search. Education in this field and good working liason are the only answer.

Break and Enters

The best method of deployment for area containment is to place a patrol car in a position where the officer can see if someone crosses the roadway from the point of entry. If a point of entry has been located and the suspect has left within the last few minutes, the perimeter of containment should be widened. Place cars at corners where officers can observe two or three blocks in two directions (if on the corner of the area contained) or three directions (if containing a long area.) An officer placed between two corner-containment officers can see the area in each direction towards the two corners as well as down the street which intersects through the containment area.

The primary unit on the scene should avoid bringing the patrol car too close to the point of entry as exhaust fumes (particularly unleaded gas exhaust through catalytic converters) will obliterate any ground or contact scent as well as interfere with the dog's olfactory capabilities. The fumes from the cars using converters has a long numbing effect on the PSD nose which often hampers his ability to follow relatively fresh scents.

If no suspect is seen leaving the area or the point of entry, always do a building search with the dog. Quite often the dog is sent on an area search when in fact the suspect is still hiding in the building. Very frequently, a dog will find a suspect where patrol members have already searched with negative results. If proper containment is maintained under most fair-weather conditions, a dog will be successful, given that the information received from the attending members is accurate.

If a suspect is seen running between two buildings, the officer should recall the exact spot, as the dog handler will have to start his track on the leeward side for the dog to wind-scent properly. In a slight breeze the wind scent may carry ten or twenty feet downwind. This must be kept in mind as patrol members move through the area — avoid mixing additional scents with that of the suspect.

It is important that the information obtained from witnesses be as accurate as possible. Often hysterical witnesses will state the direction in which they think the suspect went, rather than simply indicating the exact spot where the suspect was last seen. A dog team loses valuable time trying to locate the scent when in reality it is in an entirely different location.

Armed Robberies and Violent Crimes

Dogs can be utilized to area-search for discarded clothing, weapons, disguises and so on. These can be invaluable for evidence and investigation. Often stolen articles are buried or hidden for later recovery; these items can easily be picked up by a well-handled dog. Again the rules are the same. Speedy containment, coordination of units and exact information for the handler are vital.

For street survival tactics a patrol member should be assigned to the dog team as an escort. This provides cover for the handler during armed suspect calls, as he cannot arm himself and properly prepare against a sudden attack while concentrating on his dog. The escort also works as a takedown man in situations in which more than one suspect is encountered. Once the first suspect is located, the escort officer takes custody of him, enabling the handler to proceed to track the second suspect. The escort officer can also be used as the exhibit officer when evidence is located on the track. He is able to retrieve the items firsthand and give appropriate evidence if required.

Property Recovery

As previously mentioned, suspects may bury or hide articles in dense bush areas for recovery days later. Drug caches are left at drop sites and stolen property is hidden and camouflaged. In these cases the dog can be of assistance, as he is able to seek out articles which are foreign to the natural environment.

Building and Area Searches

The dogs are trained for building and area searching. They do this by attempting to locate the fresh scent of a person hiding in the location. A fully-seasoned dog will be aware of a scent indicating fear.

Follow the same procedures of containment as that for break and enters — the only difference is that the perimeter should be closer to the building being secured, with officers able to watch two sides of the premises from a corner if necessary. Should the suspect escape, the perimeter should be widened as in the B&E procedures.

If it is believed that the suspects are within the building, allow the dog to enter first. He will pick out any human scent and indicate it to you far sooner than if you were to attempt to physically search the building.

In large fields the same containment procedures apply. Where at all possible you are to contain the area from the possible escape of the suspect as well as from contamination by other people.

Keep in mind that the denser the grass or bush, the stronger the scent; the lower the evaporation rate, the longer the scent will linger.

Questions and Answers

Q. Can a PSD scent a suspect out of a lineup after picking up the scent at the crime scene?
A. No. this is a common fallacy. There is a theory that this type of scent discrimination is possible and it has been experimented on with varying degrees of success, but it is not effective enough to warrant the use of dogs in this respect.

Q. Can a dog track over water?
A. No. The scent spreads rapidly over water and dissipates quickly. However, the scent will hang close to the bank of a river for long periods of time, providing a point of entry into the water as well as a point of exit on the opposite side.

Q. What are the most favorable conditions for using the dog?
A. The best situation is where the dog is able to work downwind and the earth is warmer than the air. Any sudden fall in air temperature enhances the scent, as does the presence of moisture.

Q. Can a dog track when it has rained?

A. If it is raining hard the scent may be obliterated, depending on the extent of the rainfall. However, in light rain, or if the ground is moist and it has stopped raining, the scent may be enhanced and will last longer than if the same terrain were dry.

Articles of Interest

— Experiments prove that the earth "breathes." Scent is good when the earth is exhaling and poor when inhaling. The earth exhales when its temperature is higher than that of the air, and inhales when cooler than the air.

— Dogs which seem not to be following the track because they are many yards downwind are actually following the scent as it is carried by the wind from the quarry.

— Crushed grass caused by a suspect running across a field will produce very good scent. Grass crushed during a frost will produce no scent.

— The scent of grass juices is not affected by sunlight.

— The individual scent of a man is carried by his sweat. This individual scent vanishes after four to five hours of bright sunlight.

— Frost checks scent, but this scent will reappear as the frost begins to melt. The same holds true for snow. Both lock the scent in, but release it during thawing. This is a valuable fact which is rarely made use of. Tracks "frozen" into frost or snow can be utilized successfully many hours after the event when thawing begins and the scent is subsequently released and enhanced.

— Man gives out a peculiar scent when alarmed, scared, or in other states of high emotion. This scent is very distinctive to the dog and is often referred to as fear scent.

Car Accidents Involving the Dog Unit

With the ever-increasing rate at which dogs are being called to crimes, there is a high risk of the K9 car being involved in a serious motor-vehicle accident.

Situations have occurred where emergency units arriving on the scene are unable to assist the K9 officer because he is trapped inside his vehicle and his K9 partner, confused and excited by the accident, is protecting his handler from those who are there to help him. Needless to say, this makes for some tense situations. In some cases the dog has been destroyed by another officer so that entry could be gained to the vehicle.

This type of tragedy can be avoided in almost every situation. If you as a patrol officer attend the scene of a motor vehicle accident involving a dog unit, have dispatch contact another dog man immediately. He is the most capable person to contact and may be able to give you instructions which will help you considerably.

On your approach to the car ascertain if the dog handler is still conscious and tell him to close the separator between the front and rear compartment.

If the officer is unconscious you can usually gain access to the front compartment of the car long enough to reach in and close the separator by having a second officer tease and distract the dog from the opposite direction. Should it be necessary to remove the dog from the vehicle, the officer's wife or another family member familiar with the dog should be contacted and brought to the scene. There is usually someone close to the officer who is also capable of handling the animal.

Remember that common sense prevails in such circumstances, that the animal is very much a part of the handler's family and is his best friend on the road, not to mention what the dog is worth to the department in training costs. He will be confused and scared in such a situation, so stay rational. You will likely arrive at a successful conclusion for which your dog man will be eternally grateful.

14
Stress and
the Police Service Dog

This chapter is to help you to understand the types of physical and emotional stress which play major roles in the physical and mental makeup of your dog. As mentioned in previous chapters, we often find dogs which act abnormally in given situations, such as the dog who is normally a gentle animal, yet given the proper set of circumstances will bite a small child. This chapter should assist you in understanding why these incidents sometimes happen, how to foresee and recognize the problems of stress in your dog and how to alleviate some of these.

Police officers themselves withstand large amounts of stress on the job. There are long periods of time in which there are simply very few or no calls to answer, during which the officer becomes relaxed. At some point during this relaxed state he may suddenly observe a burglary in progress or be called to handle an armed robbery in progress. His adrenalin starts to flow, the heart rate increases, he starts to think ahead about the scene he is heading towards and to decide how to handle the call in a manner which exposes him to a minimum of risk yet will still contain and capture any offenders.

Upon arrival at the scene, the officer either encounters his suspects, in which case the tension continues to mount and is sustained until the conclusion of the situation, or he learns that it is a false alarm. He begins to relax, the heart rate returns to normal and he continues with his routine duties.

This is a simple example of stress. Add to this single event such conditions as marital or financial difficulty, a recent death in the family or other problems of stressful nature, and you have the makings of an unreasonable, moody, and possibly dangerous man.

A man who is experiencing stressful periods in his life must take the time to slow down and sort out his problems one step at a time in an effort to regain order and control. No matter how simple or complex the encountered stress may become we are still able to formulate ways in which to handle each individual situation.

Your partner has the same capacity to be affected by stress in his job. This stress can make him seem to grow old quickly; he may become irritable and begin to lack enthusiasm. Perhaps he starts to shake uncontrollably, or suddenly demonstrates anxiety in certain situations. These can be signs of stress in different degrees.

Stress is tested in the police serve dog during the first few weeks of life; the tests conducted when the puppies are first being selected from the litter are, in fact, stress tests.

When the pup is first taken from its mother and placed in a new environment, he suddenly finds himself without the mother's warmth, with no familiar brothers and sisters, and no convenient source of nourishment. Even the sights, sound and scents in the new area all are different. As you watch the puppy, you observe him to see if he will investigate his new surroundings with interest, or simply whines, cries, and attempts to return to the mother. The pup which reacts by investigating the surrounding area and has no apparent problem adjusting to his new situation shows an excellent ability to adapt to stress.

By playing and rough-housing with the pup, by pinching a toe and causing him some discomfort, we again increase his level of stress. The length of time it takes him to adjust to these and other situations, as well as how he adjusts determines how he is rated. The pup which adjusts easily, is quick to forgive and trusts you in unusual surroundings and situations shows good ability to withstand stressful situations and is a preferred candidate.

While you are raising your puppy, be watchful for incidents which may indicate an inability to withstand stress. Such situations will vary, but are easily recognizable if you know your partner well. Serious consideration should be given to replacing the puppy should any such indications appear. During the course of your work on the streets, the amount of stress encountered will increase as your dog's ability to handle calls improves. You and your fellow patrol members will expect more of him as his experience increases, and both the ever-increasing crime rate and the growing confidence in your teamwork will result in a greater call load.

Unlike the dog in training or in its first year on the streets, your experienced dog will encounter more violent suspects, and will be used to quell violent situations on a regular basis. The suspects involved will not be quite as gentle or cooperative as the quarries your dog trained with. He will encounter more physical resistance in the form of suspects with knives, guns, clubs, and even crowbars and tire irons. He will constantly be teased, out of their simple ignorance, by pedestrians who happen by your parked patrol car.

For these and many more reasons we must work hard first to choose a partner with a calm and controllable temperament, and then to raise the puppy to have the type of personality we desire. This is accomplished via the bonding process, when we instill the basics of trust and control into the animal. Third, while he is maturing we must continually scrutinize him for his ability to handle stress.

An animal which shows signs of breaking down under stress will be unpredictable, unreliable, and potentially uncontrollable in vital situations.

Therefore all effort must be taken to weed out potentially problematic pups during the early stages of bonding and training.

During a recent training program a candidate dog which had excelled in the basic tests was found to break down when training on the agility course. When faced with jumps and obstacles which challenged his balance and agility, he started to shake uncontrollably. The dog was more than capable physically of completing these tasks, but mentally he was "stressed out" to the point where he was incapable of performing. The dog was dropped from the course and replaced with another candidate animal which successfully completed all phases of training.

Had this particular dog been worked on to improve his confidence, he may have eventually improved somewhat, but not to the degree where a police officer would want to depend on him in a life-or-death situation.

Stress on the Street

As you react physically and mentally enroute to a call, so does your partner. He has learned that when the speed of the patrol car increases, or when there is a burst of the siren, he is likely going to get to work. He will stand up and show excitement by barking or pacing in the rear of the car.

These external signs are accompanied by mental and physiological changes as well. The blood pressure and heart rate increase as the dog

anticipates the coming action. His increased mental activity and the resulting physiological changes all serve to increase the dog's stress level.

To effectively handle situations he then encounters, the dog must be able to handle the stress of the anticipated action as well as that of the tracks, obstacles, and possible violent encounter with the suspect. Throughout the incident he must remain confident and reliable.

Should you reach your destination and canine assistance is not required, the dog's anticipation will remain high until he realizes he will not be used. From this point the adrenalin flow decreases, in turn decreasing the blood pressure and heart rate. I believe that in each circumstance where the dog is not used he feels a sense of disappointment, much as if you had offered to play "fetch" and after working him up into a playful mood you suddenly put the ball away and refuse to play.

During each shift, you and your partner may possibly encounter eight or ten calls, and the resulting decision as to whether to use the dog varies with each call. Unlike working with a quarry where you can control whether or not the dog gets his bite, you may go for days with incomplete tracks, or with calls where your partner is never needed to assist. Such are the circumstances of the job. Your partner must be able to withstand the pressures of constant variation. Added to the normal stress of individual calls are the instances described earlier, where people in their ignorance intentionally tease the dog as they walk by the squad car. The combination of such factors results in the potential for your partner to become "stressed out" by constant, sudden changes in aggression and activity levels.

You must be aware of the effects of stress on your partner and do your best to help him handle this stress. Failure to do so may cause an excellent working dog to "burn out" two or three years earlier than his normal retirement age. Easing the pressures of the job on your partner is actually an easy task; there are a few very simple things you can do to decrease the stress on the dog and fulfil his desire to please you at the same time.

First, once you have completed training and have hit the streets, your dog will require just as much rest as you will between shifts. His kennel at home should be situated in a rather secluded area where he will not be distracted by outside influences. He must be able to rest sufficiently and know that he can relax fully without having to be prepared for anything. He needs time away from the interference of your children as well. Therefore if you are sleeping during the day between nightshifts it may be advisable to bring the dog into your room to rest. This ensures that he will not be bothered and can rest adequately for the following nightshift.

Second, maintain his health and see that he is fed as regularly as clockwork. Shiftwork can play havoc with the dog's physiological functions as much as it does with man's. If his sleeping, feeding and activity patterns are irregular, you will be placing unnecessary stress on his physical health.

Third on the list is to stabilize his rate of activity on the streets with some form of playtime after an incomplete call. His anxiety has built up while enroute, and he is very willing to work. You can fulfil his need to complete the task by playing with him after an incomplete call. A game of tug of war, fetching a ball, or a short area search or track once in a while will do wonders to vent the dog's anxiety. He will also learn that every incomplete call is not necessarily a letdown. Keep the exercises simple and short so that you are fulfiling his desire to complete the task without making him work too hard. This is a type of cooling-down exercise and we don't want to keep his stress level up or wear him down so he will be unable to work adequately on a difficult or lengthy call. On the contrary, we are using this activity to calm and relax him.

Finally, on your days off spend enough time with your partner to maintain his skills and to fulfil his desire to work for you. Exercises and playtime perform a very important role in your partner's life. Both give him a sense of purpose and allow you to maintain the bond between you. This activity is also a source of relaxation for the dog on his off days as a game of golf or a tennis match may be for you. On these off days he learns that he is among friends and does not need to prepare to combat a potential adversary. This time off will do wonders to alleviate stress on your partner.

You are dedicated to your work with your dog and he is likewise dedicated to you. Follow the instructions given in this chapter and be aware of stress on your partner; it is something which you can understand and partially control. Proper understanding and prevention can ensure a long, comfortable working life for your partner. Should you encounter problems which are difficult to handle or understand, visit your veterinarian for assistance. He is always your closest and most reliable source of help.

15
Courts
and the K9 Officer

Qualifying as an Expert Witness

As daily crime statistics increase, so does the use of more versatile methods of law enforcement, in this case the dog. Initially it was fairly easy to go into court and explain how the dog was able to track the accused, but now we encounter lawyers who specialize in this field, just as there are those who specialize in cases involving the breathalyzer for drunk drivers. They take the time to learn every aspect of the science of smell in the dog and know the animal's capabilities and limitations. Now more than ever you must know precisely what you are talking about when you take the stand or you may find yourself in a very uncomfortable situation. You may know you have the right man, and you know there was a continual track from the crime scene to where the suspect was arrested, but are you capable of showing the reasons why and how you were able to conclude that your dog was on the right track?

This short chapter will give you some points you should keep in mind as your training and experience progress. Most of all I hope it encourages you to continue learning as much as you can about our K9 friends.

I would encourage every member of a K9 unit to join his regional or national police K9 association and attend the activities whenever possible. This will enable you to keep up-to-date on the latest discoveries and training methods and to share information with your peers on a first-hand basis. Through ongoing study and activities, your accrued knowledge will enable you to be totally conversant in the field of police service dogs and their application. Armed with proper knowledge and experience, you will feel confident with the court process.

Use of dog tracking evidence is widely accepted in today's courts. There are two basic evidentiary rules which apply to qualification as an expert witness in the K9 field:

1. Anyone with specialized knowledge may testify if it is relevant to the case for the prosecution or the defense.

2. Statements made by the handler must qualify him as well as his dog. In this respect the following must be proven:
    (a) The handler is qualified to use the dog.

(b) The dog is adequately trained to track humans. (This must be supported by actual successful tracks made by the dog. For this reason I strongly recommend the use of a "dog log" as described in Chapter 17.)

(c) The dog was placed on the track under circumstances which showed where the suspect had been. That is, continuity of track from the crime scene to the accused, or to evidence implicating the accused, such as a discarded weapon with fingerprints.

(d) The trail was not contaminated to the point where the dog could not possibly have been used effectively.

Corroborative evidence is required in dog evidence cases. Although this may be difficult to obtain, it has been shown that only slight corroborative evidence is required.

Track as Evidence to Obtain a Search Warrant

A track from the scene of a robbery to a particular residence is in itself sufficient to obtain a search warrant for the residence. The handler can act as informant, supplying the necessary information while the residence is contained by patrol members and a warrant to search obtained. In Canada this refers strictly to warrant for property, not people. This rule may vary in each jurisdiction in the United States according to individual state case law.

Use of Force

A dog is considered minimum force when used within the confines of the Criminal Code and of properly-defined departmental policy and procedure manuals.

When to Use the Dog for Apprehensions

1. On indictable or felony arrests for fleeing suspects.

2. When the proper deployment of the dog can be used instead of a gun.

3. When necessary to reduce danger to crowds during apprehension of armed suspects.

There is no criminal or civil liability to the officer when the dog is utilized and deployed within the guidelines of the "Use of Force" sections of the Criminal Code.

Your reports should be written in very detailed, factual form. Do not omit anything. Describe the incident step by step, giving complete description of directions, turns, evidence or property recovered, where and when.

Make entries in your dog log after each and every track. Make sure each entry is complete so that it can be used as evidence in court. Include weather and any unusual circumstances. If you keep this dog log up to date it can establish your credibility vs. liability in court. (Liability is described as the ability of defence counsel to break down the evidence.)

Remember, as previously mentioned, specialized lawyers are becoming more common and you will find that most defence lawyers are more knowledgeable than the prosecutors.

In Court

1. Take your dog log and success statistics.

2. Report your abilities and qualifications, background on association memberships, seminars, training, and so on.

3. Explain how scent works — keep it simple and straightforward. What is scent? Where are the scent glands? How is the dog able to pick it up?

4. Explain where the track started and what evidence you had that the suspect had been there. Where was the suspect last seen? What corroborative evidence is there? (e.g., witness observed suspect at the point where the track began).

5. How did you conduct the track?

Cross-Examination

Lawyers will attempt to make you feel you don't know what you are talking about. Remember they are only doing their jobs. Be confident and thorough, to the point where you don't have to grasp for answers. Be cool, knowledgeable and don't get rattled. Be able to communicate on a technical level.

As a matter of interest, in those cases where dog-tracking has led to an arrest, the correct suspect has been apprehended 98.5 percent of the time.

Evidence of confirmation tracks may also be required for court. These are logged as unsuccessful tracks. They are tracks which are tracked by the dog, but where the suspect evades immediate arrest by the use of a vehicle, weather conditions, crowds, and so on. This is the point where the track terminates.

If you lose a case because of your presentation of evidence or a defence counsel's successful cross-examination or argument, make a note of your omission and see that the gap is filled for future court appearances. Remember, case law will be continually created as the use of dogs in the field of law enforcement becomes more common, and it is up to you as a K9 officer to keep your standards of knowledge high.

Above all, don't go into court with a weak case, especially as far as your track evidence is concerned. Should you lose such a case although you know you have the right man for the offence, poorly-presented evidence and a subsequent acquittal make for a bad case. A bad case results in bad case law, and these decisions make it more difficult for other dog handlers to qualify certain evidence in future trials.

16

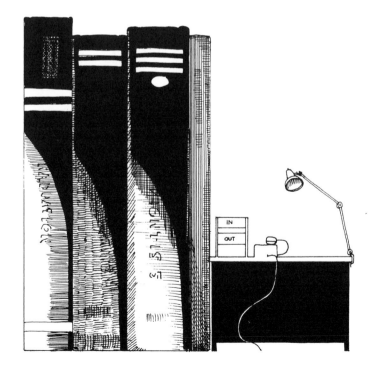

16
Administration
and Reports

The maintenance of proper statistical data within the K9 unit serves multiple purposes. First and foremost, it provides a system by which you as a handler can observe patterns in your partner which indicate weaknesses in your performance as a team, so that those problems can be identified and worked on.

Second, these records constitute accurate, specific documentation which can be used as evidence in court.

Third, to the administrators or officer in charge of the dog unit they are an important source of statistical data which can be used to justify the costs and manpower required. The NCO in charge can also easily detect patterns of successes or failures connected with each team and thereby give proper direction to improve the production of the unit as a whole.

Finally, medical records on each dog, as well as documentation of medical treatments given to suspects apprehended by a dog, provide accurate details which can be vital in the event of questioned civil liability.

Dog Log

The "dog log" is an extremely valuable tool to the dog handler. It can be kept in any hard-cover lined notebook with a large number of pages.

The log should be divided into various sections with the first section being devoted to *Training*. Here, the date and times of training can be logged in the margin and the page can be divided into two columns by drawing a line down the centre. On the left side next to the date, the training activities should be indicated and the right side can be used for remarks. Another column should be used for noting weather conditions.

The next section of the log should be for *Complete Tracks*. These are tracks which result in the successful apprehension of suspects or in property recoveries. The details of the track, including route and surfaces covered, should be accurately detailed in the remarks column as it may be significant in court should the case come to trial. Divide the pages of this section into columns for the date, track details, and file number of the case, and names of those arrested. Notations under "Remarks" as to arrests or property recoveries need not be extensive, as these are cross-referenced to those sections of the log.

Of great importance in this section as well as in the section on *Incomplete Tracks* are columns for the time of the occurrence (T/O), time of your arrival (T/A) and weather pattern (WX). You will find that over time, a pattern will develop whereby your success rate drops off dramatically in cases invloving specific weather conditions or unusual or hard surfaces, or after a certain length of time has elapsed between the time of occurrence and your time of starting the track. Once you see this pattern emerging you can start to work in those specific areas to increase your success rate. Often, quite simple problems are resolved by referring to the dog log in this manner.

Arrests is the next section of the log. These pages should have columns for the date and time, names of the accused, the case file number, and the officer who took the accused into custody. Give any details of the arrest procedures which you may need to recall for court. Indicate in your remarks whether medical treatment was required by the suspects and whether a dog bite report was filled out.

Property Recovered is a section which is largely the same as the *Arrests* section of the log. Instead of entering the name of the arresting officer, enter the name of the exhibit officer, what specific items were recovered, exactly where and in what relation to the track they were found. Have a column indicating the approximate value of the property. This can be a valuable tool at budget time when you can give accurate details of property value recovered as a direct result of K9 activity.

Drug Seizures would be the next entry of the log. Again, details of the find, type of drug and value should be entered along with the case file number and exhibit officer's name.

Next comes a section on *Building Searches*. Again, columns should indicate date and time, case file number, and names of those arrested, if any.

Each of these sections can be cross-referenced to one another if required. For example, you track from the scene of a burglary, recover property enroute and subsequently arrest a suspect at the end of the track. You would enter your date, file number, T/O, T/A, WX, and track details in the section *Complete Tracks*. Details of the property recovered and its value would be entered with the same file number in the *Property Recovered* section, and details on the apprehension of the suspects would appear in the *Arrests* section.

This method of logging dog activity may sound complicated, but in practice is quite simple and is very beneficial for court, administrative or training purposes.

The final section of the log and the largest as well is that on *Incomplete Tracks*. Regardless of how good you are as a dog team, the larger portion of entries will be in this section. You will be called to scenes which are heavily contaminated, you will track during inclement weather conditions, or the time delay between the time of the offence and your time of arrival may be so great that your chances of success are next to nil. The tracks may end where the suspect entered a vehicle, or you may be asked to do an area search as a last-ditch effort many hours after the original occurrence.

These are just a few of the many reasons why we encounter incomplete tracks. Proper entry into the log can show you areas where your dog may be having specific problems you may be capable of solving.

A log which shows many entries for incomplete tracks does not by any means indicate a poor working team. On the contrary it shows an officer who is diligent in keeping his log up to date; every dog call attended by the team should be entered in that team's log.

The dog log should be titled with the handler's name and the name of his K9 partner. It should be kept up to date and used in addition to or in lieu of the officer's standard notebook. It is a valuable aid to the officer and can be tailored to the specific needs of specialist teams as well.

Daily Activity Report

The daily activity report is a daily analysis of the activities done by each team. This report names the team, the area worked, shift times and an rundown of the day's weather. The number of calls attended to, number of arrests, property recovered and its estimated value, successful tracks, unsuccessful tracks, number of calls to assist or back up other officers, number of robbery, burglary, rape, prowler, or other violent crimes should all be entered in the appropriate column along with the file number of each case and an indication of whether the dog was or was not used in each circumstance. This will facilitate an accurate accounting of the unit's activities which can be recorded for monthly statistics. These records can easily justify the budget expended on the unit and may show where more funds should be utilized to expand the unit.

Dog Bite Reports

A dog bite report should be filled out in every case where a suspect is apprehended by a K9. The report should contain a record of the location of the bite on the suspect, treatment rendered, and the name of the doctor giving treatment. Tetanus shots are recommended in any case where the bite breaks the skin. In any circumstances where medical treatment is required, this report will show that said treatment was given as soon as practicable and is a protection in the event of a claim for civil liability due to negligence.

Dog Medical Report

This is a form used to record treatments given to the K9 should he sustain any injuries. It should be formatted with the assistance of your department's veterinarian, and used to keep an accurate medical record of all vaccinations, medical treatments and specific expenses. This record enables the administration to keep an accurate accounting of annual medical expenses so that upcoming budgets may be estimated. It is also a protection in the event of civil liabilities where a subject who has been apprehended by a dog claims he is stricken with a disease as a direct result of the dog bite.

Track Report

The track report is used as a training aid to the handler, and can also indicate to the training officer where the team is having a specific problem. In the track report, the weather conditions, time the track was laid, time the track was started, and the type of surfaces tracked are all entered. On the opposite side of the page a full-size, squared-off graph is drawn. The handler draws the route taken by his dog, the location of any turns, and any other information which seems pertinent. After the sheet is completed by the handler, the quarry (using a different color of ink) enters a sketch of his exact route taken. When the two are compared, the handler can see how his dog is following the scent, where he ran into problems, and if any particular surface type adversely affects his dog. This report should indicate wind speeds and direction. Kept over a period of time, these training aids will show a pattern in the work of your dog. You will also see specific areas in which your dog has difficulty and you can then concentrate on improving them.

Remember that a system of record-keeping can be designed to fit your specific needs. The examples I have mentioned are the kinds of forms I have dealt with in the past. Your department may desire record formats which are more detailed or less statistically-oriented; these can be generated accordingly.

These documents are all valuable tools for court purposes, and should be used to their best advantage to protect the officer and to serve the judicial system with the most accurate and detailed information possible.

EDMONTON POLICE DEPARTMENT
PATROL DIVISION – TASK FORCE SECTION
DOG UNIT
MONTHLY ACTIVITY REPORT
FOR THE MONTH OF _____ , 19_____ .

INDIVIDUAL MEMBERS MONTHLY ACTIVITY REPORT [ ] [ ] UNIT TOTAL MONTHLY ACTIVITY REPORT

NAME	RANK:	REG. NO.	P.S.D.

* NOTE *= MONTHLY AND YEARLY TOTALS TO BE COMPLETED ONLY IF REPORT IS FOR UNIT TOTAL

ACTIVITY	NO.	DU	DNU	MAN HRS.	O/T HRS.	MONTHLY TOTAL 19___	19___	YEARLY TOTAL 19___	19___
BUILDING SEARCH									
AREA SEARCH									
DRUG SEARCH									
TRACKING									
CROWD CONTROL									
STAND BY									
COMPLAINTS INVEST.									
COMPLAINTS ASSIST									
TRAINING									
COMMUNITY RELATIONS									
ZONE LIAISON									
OFFICE ADMINISTRATION									
EQUIPMENT MAINTENANCE									
DOG CARE									
KENNEL DUTIES									
STAKEOUT/SURVEILLANCE									
COURT ATTENDANCE									
GENERAL PATROL									
RECOVERED PROPERTY (INCLUDE VALUE)									
REPORT WRITING									
TOTAL KILOMETERS									

ARRESTS	DU	DNU	SUMMONSES	DU	DNU	OTHER ACTIVITY	DU	DNU
CRIMINAL			CRIMINAL			WARRANTS EXEC.		
TRAFFIC			TRAFFIC			CRIM. INTELL.		
OTHER			OTHER			TRAFFIC TAGS		
						APPREHENSIONS NO CHARGES		

DAILY ABSENTEE	CST.	SGT.		CST.	SGT.		CST.	SGT.
OVERTIME			W.C.B.			OTHER LEAVE		
VACATION			L.W.O.P.					
SICK LEAVE			COMPASSIONATE LEAVE					

15-690
601-3348A

DU = DOG USED   DNU = DOG NOT USED

GENERAL COMMENTS:

SIGNED: _____

MEMBER i/c DOG UNIT

_____

MEMBER i/c TASK FORCE

EDMONTON POLICE DEPARTMENT
PATROL DIVISION – TASK FORCE SECTION
DOG UNIT
DAILY ACTIVITY REPORT

NAME		RANK	REG. NO.	P.S.D.
DATE/DAY	HOURS OF DUTY		OVERTIME	
CAR NO.	KILOMETERS	CONDITION	ZONES PATROLLED	

SUMMARY OF DAILY ACTIVITIES:

DISPATCH & RESPONSE TIMES

R	TO	TR	TD	TA
		ONLY IF DOG USED		

WEATHER CONDITIONS – TEMPERATURE: WIND: **RELATIVE HUMIDITY:**

SIGNATURE: **APPROVED BY N.C.O. i/c:**

601 2874C
15-692

R	=	RADIO DISPATCHED	TO	=	TIME OCCURED	TD	=	TIME DISPATCHED
TA	=	TIME OF ARRIVAL	TR	=	TIME REPORTED			

ACTIVITY	NO.	DU	DNU	MAN HRS.	O/T HRS.	COMMENTS
BUILDING SEARCH						
AREA SEARCH						
DRUG SEARCH						
TRACKING						
CROWD CONTROL						
STAKEOUT/SURVEILLANCE						
COMPLAINTS INVEST.						
COMPLAINTS ASSIST					·	
COMMUNITY RELATIONS						
ZONE LIAISON						
TRAINING						
OFFICE ADMINISTRATION						
EQUIPMENT MAINTENANCE						
DOG CARE						
KENNEL DUTIES						
STANDBY						
COURT ATTENDANCE						
GENERAL PATROL						
FOLLOW UP						
REPORT WRITING						
MISCELLANEOUS						

ARRESTS	DU	DNU	SUMMONSES		DU	DNU	OTHER ACTIVITY	DU	DNU
CRIMINAL			CRIMINAL				WARRANTS EXEC.		
TRAFFIC			TRAFFIC				CRIM. INTELL.		
OTHER			OTHER				PROPERTY RECOVERED VALUE —		
APPREHENSIONS NO CHARGES			TRAFFIC TAGS				STOLEN AUTOS RECOVERED		

DU = DOG USED   DNU = DOG NOT USED

GENERAL COMMENTS:

Conclusion

The training of an efficient dog team is a lifelong endeavor, and the tasks you and your partner undertake are limited only by the scope of your imagination. There is a solution for almost every conceivable problem you will encounter. You must learn and accept your partner's limitations; once you fully understand his needs and abilities there is virtually no job you will be unable to perform as a team.

As you progress, the basics of dog training taught in this book — control, patience, adequate repetition of exercises, consistency, respecting the dog as an individual — will remain the key to mastering new challenges. In continuing to strive for excellence, you assure an effective, challenging and rewarding partnership for yourself and your K9 companion.